739314 kw

D0480625

ONE DOG, HIS MAN AND HIS TRIALS

ONE DOG, HIS MAN AND HIS TRIALS

Marjorie Quarton

FARMING PRESS

First published 1993

ISBN 0 85236 253 6

A catalogue record for this book is available
from the British Library

Some of this material
appeared in *One Dog and His Man* (1984)
and *One Dog and His Trials* (1986),
published by Blackstaff Press.

Published by Farming Press Books
Wharfedale Road, Ipswich IP1 4LG, United Kingdom

Distributed in North America by Diamond Farm Enterprises,
Box 537, Alexandria Bay, NY 13607, USA

Cover design by Paul Young
Line drawings by the author

Cover photographs by Julie-Ann Holmes
and Derick Garnier

Typesetting by Galleon Photosetting, Ipswich
Printed and bound in Great Britain by The Alden Press, Oxford

FOREWORD

I met the Boss at a sheepdog trial in Co Galway. After watching a nearly perfect run by two of the best dogs in the country he remarked, 'Well, I haven't seen anything my Shep and Dolly couldn't do.' With that, he mounted his bicycle and rode away.

This set me thinking about Shep and Dolly – and about my own collies at home – and so a story came to be written. It will make you laugh because a dog's efforts to understand human thoughts and reactions have to be laughable. Sheepdogs have been bred for one kind of work for hundreds of years, and they think in terms of work; as when they attempt to 'herd' their owners out of doors for a walk. Their mental processes are unlike those of other dogs.

'Shep' is based on my own Border Collie Ben, friend and helper for almost ten years. I even named the human hero of a novel after him. The dog on the jacket of this book is not Ben but another great working dog of mine who has also won his share of trials, named Glenn.

Glenn's honest, but slightly puzzled expression mirrors Shep's assessment of both human and canine behaviour. Shep's Man is the Boss, who can do no wrong. His trials are of many kinds – and he wins some of them.

Marjorie Quarton

For Diana

ONE DOG, HIS MAN AND HIS TRIALS

ONE

IN Coolcoffin, where I live, nearly every dog you meet is called Shep.

'What else would you call a dog?' said the Boss when the Missis asked him what name would he give me.

One thing I have that the other Sheps haven't is Papers. It's a blue card with me name and number, me Mammy and me Da's names and the Boss's as well; but he's in small letters. This number I have is 80645. It doesn't do me any good that I can see, but me Mammy told me I should be proud of it, and I am.

I don't remember me Mammy that well, though I remember her biting our ears for being bold. I think it's a pity the Boss's Mammy didn't bite his ears more when he was a pup; she might have put some sense into him.

I was born in Wicklow on the other side of Ireland. The Boss saw us advertised in *Farmers' Journal* and he took the notion to buy me because me Mammy and me Da was champions. So that's how I came to live in Co Galway, all the way in an orange-box. The farm is called Wisheen, and Coolcoffin, where the shop is and the pub, is down the road. Behind our house is Glengombeen and the Gombeen Hills beyond that. We have a lot of scenery and that kind of thing around here.

It was a bad day for me, four years ago, when I came here. For the first year of me life I hardly saw the light of day as I was kept inside in an old shed. I got as much food as I could eat and plenty of dry straw for a bed, but it was a dull old life all the same.

When I was a year old, the Boss started taking me to bring in the cows and I began to work. It came natural to me, and I thought I was doing the finest until the Boss took it into his head that he'd train me. That came to nothing, because he didn't know how and I could run faster than he could, so he gave up.

From then on, I did as I liked. I brought the cows in and rounded up the sheep; I brought in the hens for the Missis as well. It was the Missis who said I should be out in the open where I could see Life, so now when I'm not at work I'm tied to the wheel of an old trap. The Missis says I'm almost human, which she means for a compliment, the poor harmless woman. If I was human, I'd have something to do beside scratching meself and chewing this old wheel.

Indeed, until last week, I never did anything worth writing about, for it's a dog's life at times. Even my friend Dolly has more freedom than me. She's been here longer than I have and she's great for barking and chasing cars. She didn't catch one yet, but she keeps trying.

Well, the Boss went off to a sheepdog trial with Jamesy Quinn last week, and when he came home,

Shep

he told the Missis that he didn't see anything that me and Dolly couldn't do, so he decided he'd take me to the next trial, which was at Oughterard. Dolly couldn't go, on account of having puppies. They're grand little things – and why wouldn't they be? They're my puppies too – at least, I think they are.

On Sunday, me and the Boss and the Missis went off to the trial in the car. The Missis took her knitting and *Ireland's Own*, the Boss took a blackthorn stick with a crooked handle. I went in the boot, with only the spare wheel for company.

When we arrived, I lepped out of the boot and said, 'Hello, how are you?' to the first dog I saw.

He stripped his teeth. 'I'm Risp,' says he. 'I won on the telly. You watch your step, culchie.'

It didn't seem the right time to ask for his autograph, so I went under our car, had a good scratch and went to sleep.

It was in the novice class we were. The Boss hooked his stick through me collar and pulled me out from under the car. Then he led me off to the

3

start. I was a bit scared at first because I knew the Boss was shaking, but then I saw the sheep and I was all right. Anyway, I knew all me commands – Come in, Get out, Lie down damn you, Get up you useless eejit, G'way outa that and G'home you devil.

There was only four little sheep, and I wasn't long bringing them. The Boss looked a bit mad, but maybe he wasn't. I whipped the sheep around him and ran them back to the far end. Then I heard a roar, and the Boss was wanting them back again. He'd changed his mind, I suppose, and he wanted me to put them in a pen. I got them back after a while – they *did* gallop! And I put them in the pen before they knew what was happening. Then the Boss changed his mind again and let them out after all me bother.

I thought I had the trial won, but they said I did something wrong – I forget what. After that, I had to go back in the boot, so I missed the rest. I don't think much of these old trials, so I don't. And I was sick over the spare wheel going home . . .

The Boss says he's taking Dolly next time.

TWO

THE Boss isn't going to run Dolly in the trials after all. He says it's because she has no Papers – she's only a half purebred. He used to say pedigrees weren't worth the paper they were written on and he could name his dogs without sending money to any society, but that's all changed since he was talking to the experts at the Oughterard trial.

Dolly's pups are called Rover, Spot, Darkie and Ginger. They are all white with brown spots and long ears. This is funny, because Dolly is all black, and I'm black and white. One day, the Boss let the pups out to see would they gather the sheep. They didn't bring them at all; they chased them through the ditch and away to the mountain, and I had a right job to get them back. Dolly came to help me, but she just stood and barked.

At dinnertime, the Boss says to the Missis, 'Old Shep's the only dog around here that's any use.'

'Of course he is,' says the Missis. 'He's the only one with Papers.'

The Boss says, 'Begod you're right. I'll get another pedigree dog next time.' The same day, he sent away to Donegal for a new puppy. He answered an ad for a pedigree bitch pup, registration optional.

'What does "optional" mean?' says the Missis.

'It means you have to have it,' says the Boss. 'They didn't teach you much at that old convent if you don't know that.' He went off that evening to post the letter in Coolcoffin. When he was there, he called at the pub and arranged to give Rover, Spot, Darkie and Ginger to a man who was lonely. He was late back because the bike refused to carry him home. He makes out they are treacherous things after pubs.

Soon after that, the pup arrived by train in a box. LIVE PUPPY THIS WAY UP was wrote on it. The pup is called Jess and she has pink papers, which is even better than blue ones they say. When the Missis let her out of the box, she went under the dresser and screeched for her Mammy.

'You wouldn't think a pedigree dog would make such a noise, would you?' says the Missis.

The Boss went down on his knees, snapping his fingers at Jess. 'Poor little thing, she's hungry,' says he. Dolly and me thought he must be going off his

Jess

6

head. The Missis went for some milk and the Boss sat down to read his new book on sheepdog training.

These are strange times we live in.

❋

I don't think I mentioned that the Boss and the Missis have a son called Martin. He's a nice lad – a bit short of power perhaps, but we all have our faults. He's after getting a job in Tuam, so he needs the car every day and so the Boss has to make do with the bike and the Missis stays at home. She cribs about it now and then. Jess is three months old now, and doing well. So she should, with more champions in her pedigree than there's islands in Lough Corrib. Well, the Missis was at the Boss to take Jess to the vet for injections against distemper.

I was all wrong about distemper. I thought it was the stuff the Boss put on the cowshed wall. He spilled it and I walked in it – you can see the paw-marks on the flagstones yet. They are pink and I think they look lovely. Now they tell me distemper is a disease. Anyway, the Boss told the Missis she could take Jess herself if she had a grudge against her money. 'Yoke the pony and take the trap,' says he.

My wheel, what I'm tied to, is part of this trap. There's a small pony to pull it, but he's idle this long time. The Missis caught him and yoked him herself, and remembered to untie me before she took the trap out. Jess was in a box on the seat.

My wheel, where I live, isn't what it was. I have three spokes eaten right through and two half way. Well, I've been tied to it for three years, so you couldn't blame me for edging me teeth on it now and again. Anyone would.

Just as the Missis drove away, Dolly ran in front of the pony barking, the way she always does. The pony shied, the bad wheel went over a stone and that was the end of it. It all broke asunder, the trap turned over and Jess and the Missis fell out.

The Boss came flying out when he heard the row. 'Is the pup all right?' says he, picking up the box with Jess yelping inside.

'Don't mind your pup,' says the Missis. 'What about me? Look at me, all blood, and I think me finger's broke.'

I thought it would be a good idea not to be around when they looked at my wheel, so I went off for a long walk on me own.

THREE

THE Boss talks about training Jess soon. She's getting big now, and very pretty, although Dolly does not agree with me about this. The Missis thought she might train her herself, but the Boss says no pedigree dog will work for a woman. This is funny, because I work for the Missis myself. Still I suppose even the Boss could be wrong sometimes.

He is learning how to train Jess out of books. He gets them from the library and he has them all read twice. He says the best one is called *Training Sheepdogs for Profit and Pleasure*, and he reads it aloud to the Missis. ' "You must speak to your dog in language he can understand," ' says he.

'Why, you always do that,' says the Missis. 'Sometimes they can hardly get under the henhouse fast enough.'

'That's all over,' says the Boss. ' "A tone of quiet authority should be used –" quiet, mind you – "and the results will surprise you." '

'They might, I suppose,' says the Missis. 'Who wrote the book?'

'He calls himself *Come Bye*,' says the Boss. 'It says here inside the cover, "*Come Bye* exhibits an unique grasp of canine psychology." That means he understands these old dogs.' He turned over some pages and read, ' "A balanced diet is essential." '

'What's wrong with spuds and new milk I should like to know?' asks the Missis. 'Shep looks well on them.'

'It isn't Shep I worry about, it's young Jess,' says the Boss. He went off to town the same day and came back with a four-stone bag with a picture of a dog on it.

' "Collywobbles"?' says the Missis. 'What's that?'

'Balanced diet,' says the Boss, slitting the bag.

'They look more like brown wellingtons minced,' says the Missis, looking inside. Then she read off the side of the bag, ' "Just add water for meaty morsels, smothered with gutsy gravy." You'll poison the creatures.'

' 'Deed I won't then,' says the Boss. 'It's a quare name but great stuff. There's some for little 'uns too, called "Pup Slup".'

We've had 'Collywobbles' for our dinner every day since, Jess and me. The smell is a bit funny but they taste all right. Still and all, I'm jealous of Dolly eating her spuds and new milk.

Another thing the Boss found out in one of his books was that some of us sheepdogs get a disease which makes us go blind. I don't see why I should go blind. The Boss and the Missis both need glasses and I don't. But anything the Boss reads in one of those books, he has to do it, so he told the Missis he was taking me to Dublin to have me eyes tested.

'You're out of your mind,' says the Missis. 'Dublin's a hundred and fifty miles. What's wrong with Mr Finnegan in Coolcoffin?'

'It has to be Dublin,' says the Boss. 'Me and Jim Dolan will go next week.'

We went early one morning in Jim's van. I sat in the back with Ben, Jim's dog. We drove for hours and got very bored and thirsty, but at last we got to Dublin, and a vet looked at our eyes and said they were all right. It was after that the trouble started.

The Boss and Jim set off for home, but they soon stopped and went into a pub for a pint. Ben and me waited and waited. We had a small fight, just to pass the time, then we went to sleep. It was dark when Jim and the Boss came back. They drove off in great humour, singing 'Galway Bay'.

We drove for a couple of hours and then Jim says, 'Try to see the name of this big town we're coming to.'

'Wexford,' says the Boss.

'G'way,' says Jim, 'It can't be.' But it was, and it's a long, long way from Wexford to Galway, and another forty miles on to Coolcoffin.

We were home for breakfast next day. I never saw the Missis really vexed before, but this time I think the Boss would have come under the henhouse with me if he'd have fitted. It'll be a long time before he goes to Dublin again, I think.

FOUR

IT's a sad story I have to tell today. My friend Dolly is dead. This is the way it was. On Sunday, the Boss and the Missis went to a match. They left Dolly loose to mind the place, but me and Jess was tied up in the shed.

When they were gone, Martin came home with the one he's going with – she's called Julia. They found the house locked up, so they went out to the haybarn, and we could hear them talking. They were smoking too – the Boss wouldn't have allowed that. When they'd gone, we smelled smoke. Me and Jess was desperate scared; we howled and howled, but Dolly was barking at cars on the road and didn't hear.

Just then, a car came flying down our road, Dolly ran out barking and it went over her and killed her stone dead.

The driver stopped the car and backed up the road. Then he picked Dolly up and carried her into the yard and left her at the back door. Then he saw the smoke coming from the haybarn and heard me and Jess howling our best. There's a big water tank at the corner of the house, so he got a bucket and put the fire out. He let us off our chains first. I stayed to keep an eye on him, but Jess made off as fast as she could go. The fire was just out when the Boss landed back.

Dolly's funeral was to have been that evening at the river, but the Missis said it wouldn't do. She said Dolly had given her life stopping the car, so the man would put the fire out and save me and Jess and the hens from a horrible death. 'Dolly deserves a proper grave,' says she, 'And it wouldn't do you one bit of harm to dig one. You could put up a stone saying, SHE WAS FAITHFUL or something like that.'

'SHE WAS USELESS, more like,' says the Boss. 'You soon changed your mind about Dolly, didn't you? Only yesterday you were giving her who-began-it with the sweeping brush.' However, the Missis nearly always gets her way in the end, and Dolly got a fine grave at the end of the potato drills. The Missis cried, but the Boss didn't – not when I was watching, anyway.

❀

One way and another, they didn't notice Jess was gone. They were at their tea when she came back to the yard. Jess isn't used to running around loose. She began to hunt the hens into a corner and then she grabbed one and killed it. I was surprised, I didn't think she had it in her, but she made short work of that hen.

'You're in for it when they turn down the telly and hear you, my girl,' says I. 'Your pink Papers won't save you then.'

'Why?' says Jess. 'I only did what they do themselves. I just killed an old hen and took off her feathers and pulled out her insides. They often do it.'

13

'They make a tidier job,' says I.

Somewhere in *Training Sheepdogs for Profit and Pleasure* it says, 'If you feel annoyed with your dog, do not show it; keep cool and calm.' The Boss must have forgotten that – anyone could have seen he was annoyed when he came out. He grabbed at Jess, but missed and she flew off down the road.

'I used to think pedigree dogs wouldn't touch hens,' says the Missis, gathering up the bits. The Boss didn't hear her, he was calling and whistling for Jess. (He has a special whistle with a string on it so he can get it back if he swallows it.)

Then he walked all the way to Coolcoffin, shouting and whistling. And poor Dolly not cold in her grave! There's no justice in life. He took me with him in case Jess would sooner go to me than him (he had a point there.) Between shouts, he kept saying he'd murder Jess when he found her. Even so, he went to the Guards about her, and left a message with the *Coolcoffin Courier*.

We went home, and there was Jess with the Missis. The Boss looked at them, then he calmly and coolly tied Jess up. He must have remembered that old book.

Maybe the book saved Jess – although it might have been the Missis – but it'll never save us again. You see, the Boss never took it back to the library, first because he was for ever reading it, then because the cover came off, and the Missis dropped a fried egg on the chapter about 'Feeding and Hygiene' when she was giving the Boss his breakfast and he jogged her elbow.

Then one day, he saw an ad in *Working Sheepdog News* saying you could have a signed copy sent from England, and he was after winning a few pounds on a bet, so he said he'd treat himself and he sent away for it. When it arrived, he could hardly wait to tear the paper off. 'I think this is the best book ever written,' says he to the Missis as he opened it to see what was wrote inside. Then there was a silence, so I looked up to see what ailed him. The Boss was staring at the inside of the book with his mouth open.

'What's the matter, Jack?' says the Missis. 'Did he forget to sign it or what?'

'Sign it? Oh he did, he signed it, bad luck to him. He's a woman so he is.'

'*Come Bye* a woman? Are you sure?' The Missis sounded like she didn't believe him.

'Of course I'm sure,' says the Boss. 'I never heard of a man called Gwendolynne, did you? Gwendolynne Rose Hopkins.' He threw the book on the floor and stamped out of the house. The Missis picked it up and put it on top of the dresser. It wasn't mentioned since.

FIVE

WE had visitors over Christmas this year. A Scottish lady advertised for a farmhouse holiday where her own collie would be welcome, and the Missis thought it would be a great idea. 'We'll make a few bob, and Miss Cairngorm can help you to train Jess,' says she.

The Boss hadn't forgotten Gwendolynne Hopkins. 'I don't want no woman to help me,' says he, and he went off to the pub.

The Missis was extra busy getting ready for the Christmas, as she papered the spare room and did extra baking. Even so, she found time to groom me and Jess. She shined us up rightly with a Brillo Pad.

Miss Cairngorm was a big woman, nearly as big as the Boss. Her dog was big too, with long, bushy, pale brown hair and little eyes. He pretended he didn't see me.

'I know you're all going to just love Mr Teazie-Weazie,' says Miss Cairngorm, hugging him.

'We are, I suppose,' says the Boss. 'There's a chain in that shed, and some straw. You can tie him up there.'

'Oh, *no!*' says Miss Cairngorm. 'I'm afraid you need educating in doggy know-how, Mr Kelly.

16

Mr Teazie-Weazie

Teazie's used to a centrally heated kennel – he can sleep in my room.' She said most of that to herself, because the Boss had gone away.

'You aren't a Border Collie, are you?' says I to Mr Teazie-Weazie.

'Wouldn't be seen dead with one,' says he. 'No, I'm the Lassie type.'

'Oh, beg pardon,' says I, 'I thought you were a laddie. Still I suppose it takes all sorts . . .'

'Don't growl like that, my precious,' says Miss Cairngorm, 'Or Mummy will have to scold you.' Poor old Teazie, I tried not to hear. Then she says to the Missis, 'Another thing, I don't want my dog to associate with the farm dogs. He might pick something up. It's unhealthy.' The Missis went very red, but she had no chance to say anything back as the two of them went into the house.

'Mongrel,' says Teazie over his shoulder as he was led away.

❂

17

I didn't see him again until Christmas Day. He went for walks down to Coolcoffin, using the front door which I am not allowed to do. But somehow he must have given Mummy the slip, and he came walking into the cowshed just as I was finishing me Christmas dinner.

'Bit chilly for eating outdoors,' he remarked.

Now I wasn't tied up and the Boss wasn't around, so I said, 'Who did you call a mongrel the other day?'

Mr Teazie-Weazie squinted at me with his little eyes down his long nose. 'Oh, that was a joke,' says he. 'I'm proud of my ancestry, that's all. Do you know how many times my father won a green star?'

'Once in a blue moon,' says I, 'Unless there was only himself in the class.'

I'll say this for the useless looking eejit, he could fight. We fought up and down the shed and across the back yard where the pigs are, and we rolled in the channel where the muck runs away. It was a great fight and I won it. I loosed my hold of him to get a better grip and the next thing he was gone, yelping and yowling, into the house, up the stairs and, for all I know into Miss Cairngorm's bed.

The Boss tied me to the leg of the turnip pulper for two days, but I don't think he was really vexed with me. Of course, he didn't have to clean up the mess.

SIX

THE weather turned hard after Christmas, and Jess and me lived in a fine cosy stable for the rest of the winter. The cows were dry, the ewes near lambing and there wasn't much work for me.

Jess doesn't work at any time. She creeps about, a long way off the sheep, looking keen and clever, but really, she's scared. I doubt if she'd even have killed that hen if it had faced her. The Boss doesn't know she's scared; he thinks she'll make a champion some day.

One day, the vet came testing cattle, and I was hard at it rounding up the bullocks and forcing them into the crush for him. I wasn't fit, and I was glad when we'd finished.

'That's a great dog you have,' says the vet. 'But what happened to the little bitch you bought out of Donegal? Is she working?'

'I wouldn't risk a good one like her with cattle,' says the Boss. 'I'll show her to you. She's a great little mover but not ready for serious training.' He took the vet into our stable to see Jess. 'I'm going to breed champions off this lady,' says he. 'I'm sending her across the water to be mated with the International winner.'

'I'm afraid you're too late,' says the vet. 'She's already in whelp.'

'Ah, no,' says the Boss. 'I know she got stout, but that's the balanced diet.'

'It is not,' says the vet. 'It's pups.'

I was standing beside the Boss looking harmless, but I thought I'd go away. He's hasty sometimes.

Two weeks after that, Jess had five pups – real smashers. The Boss was giving out holy hell over it. The Missis says, 'I don't know why you're so vexed over it. Shep's well bred and a great worker.'

'Maybe,' says the Boss, 'But he never won a trial and I wanted big money for those pups.

You'd hardly believe what he did next. He sent me away to be trained for trials to a man who makes a business of it, so he can ask more for the pups. I never thought I'd be taking up a part time job at my time of life, but here I am at Mr O'Brien's place, being trained for trial work.

What makes me laugh is thinking how the Boss must be having to run after the sheep without me to help him. I hope he runs some fat off himself and some sense into his head.

I was handed over to Mr O'Brien at a trial at a place called Four Roads. I got talking to a dog called Mac when I got fed up with watching the trial. 'My Boss is here since eleven this morning,' says I, 'And it's getting dark. I think he's going crazy.'

'Not at all,' says Mac, 'It's sick he is. He has the Trial Bug and it's worse than distemper.'

'That's terrible,' says I. 'Will he die of it?'

'Indeed and he won't,' says Mac. My old feller's

had it for years and he's no worse. The trouble is there's no cure and it's catching.'

I was very sorry for the Boss. It's a shame when you think it could have been avoided if he'd had injections from the vet when he was young. And Mac was right; the Boss came to see me at Mr O'Brien's and from what he says he still has the Trial Bug and he's given it to the Missis.

Mr O'Brien's sheep are racing fit, ready to run for their lives. I doubt if human teeth would make much of that mutton. Mr O'Brien has two trial dogs and two students like me. One of them is called Finn, and I asked him what he was doing there after I'd seen him at work. I thought he'd very little to learn. 'I'm developing a pear-shaped outrun,' says Finn.

'Oh, God, that's bad,' says I. 'Did you see the vet?'

'I hope that's meant for a joke,' says Finn with a growl, so I said no more and I still don't know what he meant.

Mr O'Brien didn't like me at first. 'Too head-strong,' says he. 'Overruns, comes in too close, lacks the correct approach...' There was a whole pile more, but it was doggerel to me.

I got my chance when the other student, Toby, slipped his collar and made straight for the sheep, going like the clappers. The sheep took one look and bolted clean through the wire fence – Toby had frightened the souls out of them before. When Mr O'Brien caught Toby, he shook him until his brains would have rattled if he'd had any. Then he took me and we brought the sheep home, nice and handy, by the road. He's easier to work for than the Boss, because he knows what he's trying to do.

The very next day, he loaded me and Finn in a

little trailer and took us to a trial.

It was a hilly place, something like home, and there was the Boss sitting out in the rain watching bad dogs in the novice class. He still has the bug all right. 'You'll notice a big difference in Shep,' says Mr O'Brien.

'I do,' says the Boss, 'He's a lot cleaner.' While they were talking, I was enjoying myself to pieces watching the novice dogs. Some wouldn't lie down, some wouldn't get up, and one dog ran the sheep off the course, up the road and out of sight.

'These old trials are a howl, aren't they?' says I to Finn.

'You might be howling soon,' says Finn. 'It's your turn next.'

I'd learned a lot since Oughterard. I went nice and easy and minded what Mr O'Brien had taught me. When it was over, they said I had the novice class won. Mr O'Brien offered the Boss £500 for me.

'I want a thousand,' says the Boss. I didn't want him to sell me, so I nudged his hand with me nose. 'Go to hell you silly old devil,' says the Boss. It was grand to see him again and know how much he thinks about me.

The latest news is that the Boss is coming to Mr O'Brien's place to be trained himself, because he wants to run me in trials and I'm after learning different commands. That'll be a howl if you like.

SEVEN

MR O'Brien is running me in trials regular now. I've won an Intermediate class and been second twice. Twice a week, the Boss comes to be trained with me, so he can run me himself. He's not good at it, any pup would learn faster; it's because he has no patience.

Mr O'Brien set him on to penning ducks with an old dog called Kep. You have to be patient with ducks, and both Kep and the Boss found it a great strain on the temper. I'd never worked ducks, but I'm well used to putting in the hens for the Missis and you need a cool head for that. When the Missis was sick and the Boss tried it, we finished up with me under the henhouse, the Boss at the pub and the hens roosting in the sally trees down by the river.

When the ducks were penned, Mr O'Brien says to the Boss, 'I can teach you no more. It's up to yourself from now on. You have one of the best dogs in the country and I only wish you'd sell him to me.'

'I have a better at home,' says the Boss, 'when she has her pups reared and comes to her best.' He's in for a disappointment I'm afraid.

When we got home, the Boss could talk of nothing only how he penned those ducks. He thought ducks

.ould be just the thing for Jess. He talks about her not being at her best after rearing pups, but they're weaned this month back. Jess just dreads sheep, and they know it. She wouldn't go into the same field with a cow.

Our neighbour, Jamesy Quinn, has ducks. He's a bit like the Boss – cross as a bag of cats, but decent with it. The Boss asked him for a loan of the ducks.

'Fair enough,' says Jamesy. 'But don't upset them because they're laying, and my Missis will eat me if anything happens to them.'

'My dog won't hurt them,' says the Boss. 'She has the best of breeding.'

I didn't think Jamesy Quinn's ducks were worth drowning for

He let the ducks out of their crate in the middle of our big field and sent Jess after them. The ducks were afraid and began to flap their wings and quack. Jess was delighted because she'd found something that was scared of her instead of the other way around, and she began to chase them. The ducks flew up in the air and the Boss let a roar at me to head them off. I'm fast, but I can't run as fast as a duck can fly, and I was still well behind when they reached the river and set off swimming downstream as fast as they

24

were able. I jumped in and swam a long way after them, under the railway bridge and nearly to the mill. Then I said to meself that Jamesy Quinn's ducks weren't worth drowning for, and I was getting very tired.

I climbed out of the river, leaving the ducks still heading for the Atlantic, and took a short cut back to the big field. Long before I got there, I heard the Boss and Jamesy shouting at each other, so I kept to the back of the hedge and went home to find the Missis.

The Missis was very surprised to see me so wet, and she dried me with an old vest belonging to the Boss and let me sit in the kitchen.

Of course, it was the Missis who had to go down to Jamesy Quinn's wife that evening and promise her more ducks. She was gone a long time.

❉

Jess's pups were advertised in *Farmers' Journal* lately. 'Five Border Collie pups. Sire leading trial winner, dam potential champion. Unregistered due to misunderstanding. Send SAE for details.' Soon people began to arrive in our yard and go away with one of the pups. Now there's just the one left: Tiny.

Tiny is a ringing devil. He stands in the middle of the floor, bold as a pig and afraid of nobody. The Boss faults him for being small, but the Missis says even the Boss must have been small when he was eight weeks old.

Well, when the Boss came in after tying Jess up and pacifying Jamesy, the Missis wasn't back and he thought he'd go to the pub, so he set off for Coolcoffin on his bike. Tiny followed him on to the road, and I could hear the Boss trying to hunt him home. After

Tiny

a few minutes, Tiny came flying back into the yard with the Boss after him.

Now Tiny is very brave, but he knows when it's wisest not to be caught, and he ran into the shed and went under the old binder in the corner. The Boss bent down, clicking his fingers and saying, 'Come on then, good little feller.' Then he shook his fist and shouted, 'Come out of that till I skin you.' Tiny stayed where he was.

The Boss is fairly stout and not young, but he doesn't like to be beaten, so he got down on his hands and knees and began to creep under the binder.

It was a warm evening, and he was hot after the tormenting he got with the ducks, so he had no coat on him, and the next minute, his shirt got caught on the underside of the binder.

He couldn't move forward, he couldn't move back, and he was afraid he'd tear his shirt. He *did* make a noise! Tiny sat, just out of reach, with his head on one side, watching him.

When the Missis came back from Jamesy Quinn's

house, she heard the Boss roaring murder and soon found him and set him free. To make matters worse, she wasn't able to keep from laughing.

Me and Tiny spent the night under the henhouse.

EIGHT

AFTER the hay going on fire, the Boss found out that Martin and Julia were in there smoking and there was a row. So Martin went to England to look for a job there. He didn't get one, but the great thing was that the Boss had the use of the car every day, instead of only at weekends.

Then word came that Martin was coming home. 'You'd better go to Galway and get your teeth fixed first, while you have the car,' says the Missis. The Boss had teethaches cruel bad this while back, and the excuse he made for not getting them pulled was that he had no car. He's not easy to live with when he has teethaches, so the Missis kept at him and he went to Galway and had all his teeth pulled. They never pained him since.

The Boss's new teeth are a fine set, and he doesn't put them to the hardship of chewing. He keeps them in his pocket except when he wants to blow his whistle. You need teeth for whistling, so he put them in for the big trial at Manorhamilton.

I suppose I was lucky to win that trial. I work best if I'm left to meself as much as possible, and the Boss had to let me pen the sheep on me own because his whistle was mixed up with his new teeth and he could only splutter. When he has the use of his voice he shouts, and then I get edgy and so do the sheep.

The Boss hasn't forgotten all he learned at Mr O'Brien's. They laugh at this old Trial Bug, and the vets still can't cure it, but it's done the Boss a lot of good. I haven't felt his stick for six months, and I haven't felt his boot for a year.

We won the trial very easily and the Boss was solid delighted. He won a shepherd's crook and some money as well. When it was over, two strangers were talking to the Boss for a long time. They wanted to know was he going to the trial in Ballyhaunis and he said he was, then I went to sleep. I woke as they were going away. The Boss was saying, 'I want to be on the Irish team. It's me heart's desire. I won't rest until I make that team.'

'I'm sure you'll make it, Mr Kelly,' says one of the men, and they shook his hand and said goodbye.

I think he'll hardly get on the team. The National Trial is over for this year, I don't get any younger, and I don't see him winning anything with Jess. He's tried and tried to train her, and she won't even sit down when he tells her. The Missis has done much better. She has Jess trained to get the clothes pegs out of the bag, one by one, and hand them to her as they are wanted. When the Boss found this out, instead of being pleased, I thought he was going to burst with rage. He made the Missis promise not to teach me anything at all.

If Martin doesn't get his old job back, he'll be working on the farm here, and the Boss will have more time for us dogs, and the car to go to the trials.

Tiny is going to be good, if he settles down, but if Jess is a champion, I'm an Alsatian.

❈

Martin has curly red hair, and when he came home he'd grown it way down below his shoulders. He looked a holy show and the Boss ordered him to get it cut straight off, but he wouldn't. The Missis sided with Martin. 'Leave the poor lad alone,' says she. 'It's trendy he is. They have to follow the fashion.' The Boss said no more.

The Boss's hair is a patchy grey – blue merle, you'd call him if he was a dog. He hasn't any on top, but that doesn't matter because you never see him without his hat. Anyway, his hair grew and grew, and he stopped wearing his hat.

'For the love of God, will you get a haircut,' says the Missis. 'You'd frighten the crows.

'I will not,' says the Boss. 'It's trendy I am. I have to follow the fashion. I'll cut it off when Martin does.'

The next Sunday was Ballyhaunis trial and the Boss took me to it. It's a big trial and he asked the Missis would she come. 'I won't unless you do something about your hair,' says she.

'Don't so,' says the Boss.

It was me first open class and we came second. As we came off the field, who should walk up to us only the two men we saw at Manorhamilton. They shook hands and slapped the Boss on the back and took him for a beer. This time I stayed awake, and if you'll believe me, they were asking him to go in for the trial they show on the telly.

The programme is called *One Dog and his Man*.

They got the name from a song that goes:

> One dog and his man
> Went to mow a meadow.
> One dog, two dogs and their men
> Went to mow a meadow.

It's shown on Sunday evenings and the Boss and the Missis wouldn't miss it for anything.

After the Boss had his pint finished, he went to the bar to buy a round. One of the men was patting me so I stayed with him out of manners, so I heard him say to his friend, 'That old character will make the show, with his long hair and his collarless shirt and his gumboots. What a laugh.'

They arranged with the Boss for some people to go to our farm and take pictures of us all, and he couldn't wait to get home and tell the Missis. 'What? Pictures? With you looking like that? I'd be ashamed,' says she.

The next day, they took Martin and they all went to Galway. When they came back, Martin's hair was no more than an inch long – I'd hardly have known him. The Missis had her hair cut short and curly all over, like a poodle. She had a new coat and red boots. As for the Boss, if I hadn't recognised his scent, I'd have growled at him. He had a tweed hat, no hair to be seen anywhere except a few bristles round his ears, a green anorak, fawn trousers and brown shoes. He didn't look happy, but the Missis did. 'We're ready for the cameras now,' says she.

Last week, the men came to our farm to take the pictures. This isn't the trial part – that comes later, over in England. When he heard them at the door, out walked the Boss, all smiles. He had on his tweed hat and he was wearing a new Aran pullover, a check shirt and jeans. You'd have laughed if you could have seen the men's faces.

'You look very smart, Mr Kelly,' says one of them, 'but wouldn't you like to change into your working clothes? You'd be much more comfortable, and it would give the viewers a better idea of your daily round.'

'Like hell,' says the Boss, very angry. 'What, be seen by millions in me working clothes? No way!'

The man was very disappointed, but he couldn't force the Boss to change his clothes, so he had to make the best of it.

First, I was to fetch the cows, and the man was going to talk to the Boss while the cows stood around and I sat beside the Boss, looking dependable. We

Curly all over, like a poodle

have a new bull running with the cows – he's only a young one, I can manage him easily, but he never sees strangers. I saw him watching with his head down as the red van drove into the field and some men got out and started setting up cameras.

The telly man – the one we met before – says to the Boss, 'What about that bull? Is he quiet?'

'Ah, he's gentle as a child,' says the Boss. 'Is it the bull you want to talk about or me and Shep?' He was nervous, I think.

The man says in a kind voice, like someone trying to catch a dog that might bite, 'Mr Kelly – or Jack, if I may call you that – you've only been trialling for a few months, is that right? Might I ask your age?'

'Sixty-two. What age are you?' snaps the Boss.

'I hardly think my age would interest the viewers,' says the telly man.

'Then you can leave mine out of it as well,' says the Boss.

Just then, I got up, because I saw the bull pawing the ground. 'Lie down, Shep,' says the Boss, very loud and sharp because he was mad. I lay down, but I kept an eye on the bull. The next minute, he charged straight at the famous telly man. I was too quick for him and I made a spring and caught him by the nose (the bull's nose, I mean, of course).

The bull ran away, the man mopped his face with a handkerchief. 'Blimey,' says he. 'Gentle as a child, eh?'

'Now you'll have some pictures worth seeing, so you will,' says the Boss. After that, the Missis came out in her new clothes and I rounded up the hens with her, the men stayed for their tea and we parted the best of friends.

NINE

IT's hard for me to write about our trip to England. To start with, the journey is like a dream to me. The Missis put a St Christopher medal on me collar to keep me safe, and she gave me a pill called a 'Sea Leg', the way I wouldn't get sick on the boat. She made the Boss take two. When I had the pill eaten, I fell asleep and never budged till morning.

I was delighted when I saw the place where the trial was to be held, because it was a real wild spot like the hilly place where Mr O'Brien used to train me. I had to run three times and I won every time. Everything went right for me from the start, the sheep was easy handled and the Boss was whistling away without a care in the world. The Missis was so nervous, she wasn't even able to watch.

When I had only one more run to do, the final, a newspaper man came over to the Boss and asked him, 'How does it feel to be about to run in the final?'

'All right,' says the Boss.

'Are you nervous?'

'I am not.'

'Do you expect to win?'

'I might,' says the Boss, 'if I'm not pestered.'

'Oh dear,' says the man, 'I'm sorry. Here – have a drink,' and he pulled a bottle of water out of his pocket. At least, it looked like water.

'What's that stuff?' says the Boss. 'Do you want to put me drunk just when I need me wits about me?'

'Don't worry about that,' says the man. ' 'Tis mother's milk, you could drink gallons of it.' By that time, he had the top off the bottle and the smell of what was in it would knock you kicking. The Boss seemed like he'd refuse, then he changed his mind and took a couple of decent swallows.

'You should give Shep some of that,' says he. 'It's powerful stuff.' Then we went off to the start for the final.

He startled me a bit as we went, by giving a big shout, 'Up, Coolcoffin! Galway for ever!' but after that he was fine and more sure of himself than I've ever seen him. I wasn't surprised when I heard we'd won. I was more than proud of meself, and the Boss was like a dog with two tails. He shook everyone in sight by the hand (even the Missis, by mistake) and had his photo taken over and over. Mine too. It's funny when you think that a year ago he didn't know a shedding ring from a potting shed.

The newspaper man came back with another bottle of mother's milk; he'd been having some himself. 'Well done,' says he. 'Will you tell me something about your meteoric rise to stardom?'

'Could you ever leave off blethering and talk decent English, the way a reasonable man might make sense of you,' says the Boss. Then he was called over and given a fine big statue for himself. All the judges and the men who were at our farm were there, all patting me and making a big fuss of both of us.

35

'How's the bull?' says the man we knew, but the Boss let on he didn't hear him.

After that, some of the lads that was running the trial took us away in a car to go to a big dinner. It was held in the finest hotel in the town, and all the people that ran dogs was invited. The Boss was drinking pints in the bar with the other handlers for a while, then we were told the dinner was ready.

There was a man in a black suit at the dining room door and he barred the way when he saw me following the Boss. 'Sorry, sir, no dogs allowed,' says he.

The Boss turned very red. 'No dogs,' says he, 'what do you mean, no dogs? If there wasn't no dogs here, there wouldn't be no men either, or any dinner. Come on, Shep.' With that, he pushed past and marched straight into the dining room with me behind him.

I was the only dog there, so I lay quietly under the table beside the Boss's brown shoes, watching the Missis's red boots at the other side of the table, where she sat between a Welshman and a Scotsman.

It seemed a dull meal to me. All I saw of the feed was a Brussels sprout the Boss dropped – I got that. The Boss was real happy that night and when he is happy, he sings. I can sing too and so can Jess. When we lived outside we used to sing on moonlit nights: 'How Much is that Doggie in the Window?' 'The Kerry Blues', all our favourite songs. We knew dozens. The Boss didn't like us to sing at night. If you heard the bedroom window open it was time to stop. If you heard the back door open, it was too late.

When the Boss is happy, he sings a song called 'Spancilhill'. It has forty-seven verses and he knows them all. As soon as the dinner was eaten, he started.

After fifteen or sixteen verses, I got a feeling that the Missis was wanting him to stop, and I thought maybe I could help. I'm a healthy dog, so my nose is always cold and wet, and I pressed it against a bit of the Boss's leg that was showing between his trouser leg and the top of his sock. It was no good. All that happened was that he roared out, 'Lie down!' between two verses and carried on. Then I thought, well, if you can't beat 'em, join 'em, so I sat up beside the Boss and pitched me voice carefully for the high note at the beginning of the nineteenth verse. It was a bit wobbly, but dead on key and very, very loud.

That did it; everyone clapped and laughed so hard that the Boss had to stop. Then he made a speech and I went to sleep. They all had a great old time, and me with nothing but one Brussels sprout inside me, after winning the trial and all. It was after midnight before anyone thought of asking me if I wanted any supper.

TEN

IT's grand to be home again after all me travels. I'd sooner the quiet life any time, but the Boss is different – he always wanted fame.

When he was young, a long time ago, he was a great man to play football, and he never misses a match if Coolcoffin is playing. Martin, who stayed at home to mind the place while we were in England, is a good footballer too, and the team and supporters had a reception arranged for us.

The road from Dublin to Coolcoffin is long and contanglesome, so we came by train, and Martin met us at the station with the car.

Now everybody who hasn't been to school knows that there's a bridge in the middle of Coolcoffin across the river. I know that river well, because it was there I nearly drowned trying to catch Jamesy Quinn's ducks. All Coolcoffin seemed to be waiting for us on the bridge, waving and shouting.

The Boss was charmed. 'Well upon me oath,' says he, 'We have a fine welcome home,' and he got out of the car with me following. I hung back as the people crowded around us, I was in dread they'd walk on me feet. Then, all in a slap, the captain of the football team and his brother lifted the Boss up on their shoulders – all sixteen stone of him – and carried him across the bridge.

The Boss had a bad ride because Patsy Fagan is a huge big man and the brother's hardly as tall as the Missis. I thought the Boss was going to finish up in the river and he thought so too, and started to roar out, 'Let me go! Put me down!' and to use language I wouldn't like any pup of mine to hear.

I'm fond of the Boss – mad about him, I don't know why – and all of a sudden I forgot about not biting people, which is nearly as bad as biting a sheep at a trial, but not quite. I just wanted to see him safe on the ground, and so I did, though not just the way I meant.

I ran forward and bit Patsy Fagan's ankle. He was wearing purple socks and tasted dreadful. It wasn't a real hard bite, and I suppose you could say it worked. It isn't possible for anybody to stand on one leg for long with a sixteen stone angry man sitting on his shoulder. Patsy Fagan tried to do it, and they all came crashing down in a heap.

The worst of it was that I wasn't quick enough to get out of the way, and that's why I'm hopping around on three legs. The Boss has a big lump on his head and they tell me Patsy Fagan has blood poisoning.

Me Mammy told me when I was a little pup never to bite people, and she was right. No good ever comes of it.

❀

Me and the Boss went to the pub the same evening and we had a great time. There's a famous song which they sing in the pub; it's called, 'Coolcoffin

Town's the Place for me'. It was entered in a big song contest but it didn't get a prize, I don't know why. After we won on the telly, there was a new verse added, and everybody sang it for us. It goes:

> Among Coolcoffin's stalwart men,
> Don't overlook Jack Kelly,
> Who crossed the angry ocean deep
> To tangle with the English sheep
> And win upon the telly.
> Him and his faithful collie, Shep,
> They made those alien wethers lep
> And turned their hearts to jelly.

It's a great song – I wish I remembered it all.

Some of the lads were saying the Boss was drunk when he won, but he was in such a good humour he just laughed. Now if any dog likes to suggest to me that the Boss was drunk when he won, he can come and tell me so. He was as sober as anyone could be expected to be.

It was very late when we went home. All the team came too, because the Boss said the Missis would have tea made for them, but she'd gone to bed, so they went away again.

I could hear them singing all the way to Coolcoffin.

ELEVEN

AFTER we got back from England, it seemed like the Boss was never at home. He went to all the trials, but he didn't take me, because me shoulder was hurted when he fell on me on Coolcoffin Bridge. I stayed at home with the Missis and Jess and Tiny. Jess has a new lot of pups and the Missis is going to advertise them. This time she can say they have Papers, and the father won on the telly, and she says she could sell twice as many.

I spent whole days lying under the kitchen table, pondering. I used to wonder how people got some of their funny notions. What could be nicer than to be sold a pup? What better place to be than in the doghouse? What's wrong with going to the dogs? All those things are bad when humans say them. It isn't fair at all, so it's not. And whoever heard of anybody being dogged by good luck? It's always bad. I think it's time they started to talk about going to the cats for a change. Not that I've anything against cats as long as they sit still.

One day, when I was lying there thinking, a fine new car drove into our yard. There was a young one driving it, all style.

She was got up, they'd say, like a dog's dinner,

and that isn't always a compliment either. Oh, the Missis was mad! She was flour to the elbows, baking, and she had an old overall on her and slippers. She cheered up a bit when this one says she wants a puppy. The puppies are only small and the two of them went out to see them. When they came back, the Missis took down an order for one of them. 'What'll you call him?' says she. 'I have to put it down for the registration.'

'I'll call him "Fluffy",' says the young one.

'I wonder would that be right,' says the Missis. 'When he's big he'll be hairy. Tell me your own name as well, till I write it down.'

'The young woman laughed. 'Miss D. Byrne,' says she, 'and put "Fluffy" for the puppy, please. I can't call him "Hairy".'

The Missis asked her would she like a cup of tea and she said she would and down they sat. 'Please call me Deirdre,' says she. 'Everybody does. Oh, what beautiful bread. Do you always bake your own?'

Soon herself and the Missis was chattering like starlings and it came out that the Missis had made a stone of plum jam because the Boss likes it on new bread. 'He'd eat jam until it came out of his ears,' says the Missis. Then she says, 'Call me Kathleen,' and she told Deirdre how she knits Aran jumpers for the Boss because it's hard for him to fasten his shirt on account of his neck being a size nineteen.

'Fascinating,' says Deirdre. 'Kathleen, I must tell you that I write a little column for a new woman's magazine called *Herself*. Would you allow me to put in a few words about your delicious bread and so on?'

'I don't mind,' says the Missis, 'but I don't see

anyone wanting to read it.' They stayed talking a long time after that.

❊

It was a while after that when a copy of *Herself* arrived for the Missis in the post. She sat down to read it, all smiles, but soon I could see she was getting real upset. 'I never said she could put all that in,' says she, handing it to the Boss.

'What's this about?' says the Boss. ' "Kathleen, who laughingly admits to more than half a century in this remote corner of Ireland, is a plump housewife with merry blue eyes. I was sorry not to meet the redoubtable Jack Kelly, the sheepdog enthusiast, who revels in Kathleen's cooking. Mr Kelly, who takes a majestic size nineteen in shirt collars, claims that his favourite food is Kathleen's fresh, crusty soda bread, heaped with homemade plum jam." '

'She seemed so nice,' says the Missis, nearly crying. 'She asked me to call her Deirdre.'

'I'll call her Deirdre if ever I catch her here,' shouts the Boss. 'Let two women start talking, and a man can't even call his neck his own. I'll sue her for libel! I'll see her in prison!'

I got up and limped out to the cowshed for a bit of peace.

TWELVE

WOULDN'T you think that after all the stuff that was wrote about me and the Boss and the Missis, they'd have enough of fame? I know the Boss didn't like having his neck made public, but he was only delighted when there was two pages about him and me in the *Farmers' Monthly* and our picture in *Working Sheepdog News*.

Well, one morning, the Boss came down to his breakfast with his suit on, and the Missis with her hair curled up and those red boots. As soon as she had the dishes washed, she set to work and brushed me till me skin was sore. I knew there was something bad coming, and sure enough before long a young man arrived in a car. He was to take pictures for the *Coolcoffin Courier*.

For bad luck, the Boss was in a terrible humour. The Missis had made him shave and he'd cut himself, then he got his electric bill. Anyone would pity him. The Missis was all nerves, and shy with the photographer. He wasn't shy. He called the Missis 'Dear', and me 'Sheppie'. Me and the Boss hated him on sight.

'Would you like to see Shep working sheep?' asks the Boss.

'Good heavens no,' says the young man, who was called Brendan, 'I want the two of you to stand in the doorway with old Sheppie here. Put your arm around Kathleen's waist, Jack, and see if Sheppie will sit beside you, looking up at you with his soul in his eyes.'

'Dogs have no souls,' says the Boss. 'It's been proved.'

'Looking up adoringly, then,' says Brendan. I was trying not to growl. Brendan was the kind of person who needs to be bitten, but I hadn't forgotten Patsy Fagan's purple socks. I looked at me feet and just squinted up sideways when the Boss spoke to me.

'Will I get a bit of liver,' says the Missis, 'and hold it up for him?'

'NO!' roars the Boss. 'Look at me, you villain!' This was to me, of course, and I did, but not at all adoringly and with me ears laid back. 'Click,' went the camera.

I'll say this for Brendan, he had great courage, for next he asked the Boss to sit on the step with his arm around me, and the statue we won in his other hand. The Boss squatted down, grumbling, and grabbed me by the collar, while the Missis went to fetch the statue.

'Would you mind taking your pipe out of your mouth,' says Brendan, 'I can't see you for smoke.' The Missis came back with our trophy and the Boss took a hold of it and put his pipe on the step in front of me. I shut me eyes and coughed.

'Big smile now, Jack,' says Brendan. The Boss bared his teeth. 'Click,' went the camera again, and the Boss jumped up.

'That's enough,' says he. 'Take a picture of the

Missis if you want more. I have business to see to.'
He went into the house and banged the door. A
minute later, we saw him going past the gate on his
bike.

After he'd gone, things went better. Brendan got
all the pictures he wanted and away he went.

❂

They say a good dog keeps learning until he dies,
and it's a fact. A dog at a trial once told me I led a
sheltered life, and when I told him how the rain
blows in under the henhouse when the wind's in the
west, he nearly died laughing. So I learned to keep
quiet when I'm not sure of me ground.

The day we had our photos taken, I learned something else. You have to have a licence to keep a dog,
and the Missis has to have one as well. I suppose you
call it a woman licence. I must find out.

When Brendan had gone, the Missis was sitting on
the step in the sun with Jess and Tiny and me.
The pups were having a game with an old pullover
belonging to the Boss. (He didn't miss it yet.)

Around dinner time, Guard Whelan arrived on his
bike. He wanted a sitting of eggs for his wife. He
couldn't get near the door for dogs, and he tried to
push me out of his way. Guard or no guard, I wasn't
having that, and I growled to warn him.

'Shep won't touch you,' says the Missis.

'He'd better not,' says the Guard, keeping at the
back of his bike. 'How many dogs have you? Have
they licences?'

'They have not,' says the Missis. 'We never
bothered getting them.'

'You'd better start bothering, unless you want a

46

fine,' says Guard Whelan. 'I can manage not to see Shep, as long as he doesn't growl at me, but there's nine dogs here. You'll have to see to it at once.' He sounded so vexed, me and Tiny thought the Missis needed protecting, and we went and stood one each side of her, growling our best. (Jess is a pacifist.) 'Get those licences today,' says the Guard, backing away. 'I'll be back tomorrow – with the squad car.'

The Missis was in a terrible way. There was no sign of the Boss coming back, but the car was in the yard. Now the Missis is getting driving lessons from Martin off and on for the past year. Martin is a bad teacher and the Missis will never make an International Driving Champion, she's very much in dread. All the same, she said she'd drive, as Coolcoffin is a fair walk and the post office might be closed. I got in the boot as usual.

It seemed a long time before we stopped and then there was a lot of running backward and forward in jerks, like a bad dog at the pen. I found out later that the Missis was trying to back the car into a No Parking place between Colonel Crankshaft's Land Rover and a post office van. Then there was a great crash and the noise of glass breaking, and the boot lid kind of bent in on me. I was too frightened to notice much, but I heard people shouting and I felt the car rocking as they tried to open the boot. They had to call the fire brigade to get me out, and there were two Guards, writing in books. Strange ones, from Galway.

'Where's your licence?' says one to the Missis.

'I haven't one,' says she, wiping her eyes. She was crying because she'd thought I was killed stone dead in the boot.

That was how I found out that the Boss has to have a licence to keep the Missis, just like us dogs. We had a bad few hours waiting for him to come home. The Missis made an apple cake to pacify him, but she was so shook up she let it burn.

It was late when the Boss came home. I licked his hand and the Missis helped him off with his coat. 'What the hell is wrong with you all?' says he. 'And where's the car?' When he heard what happened, he was so glad we weren't hurted he didn't say much.

We all have licences now.

When the *Coolcoffin Courier* came on Thursday, the Boss looked at it and threw it on the floor. I came out from under the table to look. Right in the middle of the front page was a lovely picture of the Missis with one arm round me and the other round Jess and her lap full of puppies.

The Boss says he's changing to the *Connacht Tribune*.

THIRTEEN

THERE's no end to the things the Boss is being asked to do since we won on the telly. For one thing, he was asked to go on the committee for a Field Evening. He went off to a meeting and they all decided to run a sheepdog trial there. The Boss was highly delighted, because he was to be the judge. That would be good news for his friend Jim Dolan and my friend Ben.

The Boss missed getting the *Coolcoffin Courier* for a couple of weeks after they didn't print his picture, so it was Martin showed him a piece in it he'd missed. The Boss began to read aloud and his voice shook: ' "The Coolcoffin Field Evening committee has decided to abandon the projected sheepdog trial in place of a dog show, as the latter would have more spectator appeal. A further meeting will be held on Friday night—" I'll be there,' says the Boss, grinding his teeth. 'Spectator appeal, be the holy.'

I didn't know what a committee meeting was, but I know now, and I've even been to one and lived to tell the tale. The Boss takes me with him nearly everywhere now, but even so I was surprised when he took me to the meeting, which was in the back room at the pub.

It's hard for me to explain a committee meeting so that other dogs will understand. Try to imagine a big field with about twenty sheep in it and an open pen in the middle of it. The chairman is the handler and he has to pen them. It's hard for him, because the sheep all come from different flocks and they run all over, bleating away. Then, when they're penned, or most of them, the chairman has to make them stay inside with the gate open, and he has to persuade them that they like it there and that they chose to go in. That's bad explaining, but I'm not able to do any better.

The committee all had different notions, and when the Boss mentioned a sheepdog trial they all began talking at once. They said the field was wanted for a tug of war and a wellington throwing competition. Then when the Boss said Jim Dolan's small field would do for those, they said there was to be a beauty contest and a baby show there.

The Boss began to shout and soon they were all shouting. No one hit anyone else, though I was sure they would and I was ready to go for anyone that attacked the Boss. At last the chairman banged his glass of stout on the table and most of them stopped shouting to listen. 'As far as I can make out,' says he, 'Jack Kelly is the only man who wants a sheepdog trial. Well he can enter his dog in the show, and if it's good enough he might get a prize. There's to be a class for collies.'

The Boss jumped up in such a hurry he trod on me tail with his tackety boot. I yelped, but nobody heard with the racket going on. 'I never got such an insult in me life,' says he. 'I wouldn't be seen dead in a dog show. You'll be telling me to enter for the beauty contest next.' At that, everyone laughed and the Boss made for the door. 'Come on, Shep, we're not wanted here,' says he. 'I resign.' We went into the bar and he bought himself a whiskey.

It wasn't long before the others persuaded him back. They all like him, and said he could judge the wellington throwing instead of the trial, and give a demonstration with me.

❦

Tiny has been at Mr O'Brien's getting trained, and he brought him back a few days before the Field Evening. I could tell he wasn't happy. 'Mind this fellow, Jack,' says he. 'He could be as good as Shep if you have patience.'

The Boss went very red. 'Are you saying I'm short of patience?' says he. 'I mean to run him and Shep in braces in the summer.'

Of course every pup knows that a 'brace' is when you run two dogs together, but the Missis says, 'Indeed you will not. Nobody wants to see your braces – keep your coat on or buy a belt.'

The Boss just looked at her. 'I'll do better,' he says. 'I'll demonstrate with the two of them instead of Shep on his own.'

That week, the Boss got down to working Tiny and me together. I used to say to Tiny, 'If you can't behave yourself, you'll be sold, and then you'll be sorry.' Tiny didn't care. I think he didn't even hear the Boss roaring, although I know it's hard to believe.

Nothing would turn the Boss when his mind is made up, and off we went with a few sheep for the demonstration. He kept Tiny near him while I did

51

most of the work, but there was a fancy dress parade going on a few yards away. There was a big fat lad on a pony – he was supposed to be Brian Boru. Tiny gave the Boss the slip and chased the sheep right out of the ring. He nipped the pony on the heel as he went by. That was it; the pony bucked, Brian Boru turned the wildcat and landed in some nettles. He was still roaring when I'd fetched the sheep back. There was no sign of Tiny.

The worst of it was, this lad was the son of the chairman and it was him that had the sheepdog trial stopped. He came to our house in a right rage and accused the Boss of setting a dog on his son's pony out of spite. The Missis went to her sister's house for the evening and I joined Tiny under the henhouse.

FOURTEEN

TINY was in big trouble over biting the chairman's son's pony, and he killed two hens since. That makes eleven since Christmas. Then he chased our big ginger cat and cornered him at the back door. The Missis heard the spitting and growling outside so she opened the door, and Ginger rushed in and up on the dresser, where he broke five plates and a milk jug. Tiny, who had been working in the silage yard and was rather dirty, couldn't get up on the dresser, so he jumped on the table which was half way there. It was set for the dinner.

I'd warned him many a time and he wouldn't listen. The Boss took him to a dog sale. I wasn't supposed to go, but I jumped in the car and went along for the ride.

The sale was good for good dogs, but Tiny wasn't being a good dog that day. Him and the Boss had to give a show with some sheep, and Tiny went round them like an aeroplane. The Boss was dizzy from turning round and round. Tiny had the sheep packed around him as tight as murder, and he couldn't push his way through them. I was watching, and he had to call me to come and help.

The dogs was sold by auction and nobody wanted

Tiny. When it was all over, a small little man with broken teeth came over and asked the price. I didn't like the look of him. Inbred and badly reared, I thought, and could do with a dose. He said he was called Chris. The Boss asked £350 and Chris bid £50. 'I don't want him at all,' says he, 'except to tame him and maybe make a few bob.'

Mr O'Brien was there and he nudged the Boss with his elbow. 'Don't be in a hurry to sell,' says he. 'Tiny'll make a good cattle dog.'

'I know that,' says the Boss, 'Show him bullocks and he'll bring them, dead or alive.'

Chris went off and Mr O'Brien says, 'Watch that boyo. He lives near me and I know him well. His cheque could bounce. He's bad news.'

'So's Tiny,' says the Boss. When we were going home that evening, Tiny ate all the wires in the boot, the lights went out and the Boss got a summons.

❀

The next morning the Boss says, 'That's it. I'm going to shoot Tiny.'

'No, no,' says the Missis, 'Take him to the vet or the cruelty man; it's kinder.' They argued all through breakfast. Either way, things looked black for Tiny. I went out to the cowshed to find Jess, who is Tiny's mother, feeling very low.

After a while, the Boss came out with a dog chain in his hand and went to Tiny's shed. Then he got down and looked under the henhouse. I heard him shout to the Missis, 'Did you let Tiny loose? He's gone.' It was the usual story, Tiny had slipped his collar. I don't know how he does it. I couldn't.

They both looked all over for him (the Missis

Tiny

didn't look very hard.) 'I might as well let the cows out,' says she, and her and me went off to the field with them. The bull was in the field. He'd never been any trouble since he went for the high-up telly man.

I knew there was something wrong and I ran ahead. There was a young lad who'd been taking a short cut, I suppose, trying to get through the black-thorn hedge. The bull was diving this way and that, trying to get at him, but Tiny was hanging on to his nose like a bulldog. I ran to help him and we hunted the bull right away. The Missis took the young lad home to his Mammy and me and Tiny chased the bull into a stable.

The bull went away yesterday in a lorry. I think he went to be put to sleep by the cruelty man instead of Tiny. Tiny is in a right mess – he got tossed and walked on. He has three broken ribs and today he can hardly move.

The Missis brought him into the house, crying over what didn't happen. Of course he got away and sat down as bold as brass on the best settee. The Boss said there wasn't enough money in Ireland to buy him, and the Missis washed him with my special soap.

I am not top dog any more.

✥

Now that Tiny isn't to be sold, they talk about selling Jess. The Missis wouldn't like that because she gets the money for the pups, but the Boss complains because she doesn't do any work and eats more than I do. He's sore because he was wrong about her all this time. He doesn't like being reminded of it.

It would be dreadful if Jess was sold. She knows everything, does Jess, and she has real beauty. I know people like a different kind of looks. Martin thinks Julia's beautiful, and he's going to marry her when he gets time, but wait till you hear about Jess. It's her eyes. One is a deep brown, and the other, the right one, is a lovely milky white. You never saw anything like that on a woman, did you? I thought not.

Jess knew why the Missis gave pills to the puppies, and she noticed that she missed Tiny and dosed Nell twice. She says that's why Tiny stayed so small. It didn't do Nell any good either. The stuff the pups got was called Vermolin and I got some as well after I came back from England.

One evening when I was lying under the table watching the telly, I saw meself. Here was me and the Boss winning, then the Boss on his own holding a bottle of Vermolin. There was a song with it. 'The Vermolin goes in and the worms come out and that's what it's all about.' Then they showed me again and

56

a man's voice says, 'I'm free of parasites now,' says Shep – 'Thanks to Vermolin.'

What a thing to do to me! I'd have spat out the pill if I'd known. I never said a word about the stuff, and I may be full of parasites, whatever they are, for all I know. I hate to think what the other dogs at the trials will say. I'll never hear the end of it.

FIFTEEN

THE Boss was worried about the cost of taking me to Wales for the International Trial if we got on the Irish team. He asked Jim Dolan and Jim Dolan says, 'You need to be sponsored.'

I was puzzled. 'What's sponsored, do you know?' says I to Jess, who knows most things. 'It's either being chained up very tight or else it's some kind of an operation,' says she. I think she must have been wrong – I hope so. Jim Dolan said the Boss was to be sponsored by a Mr Flanagan.

At the pub, the Boss mostly drinks stout, which isn't too bad if you're thirsty, but at a funeral or a wedding, he drinks whiskey. I suppose it doesn't taste as bad as it smells – the smell would beat the devil out. I don't know how they drink it. His favourite whiskey is called Black Dog and is brewed in our own county by Mr Flanagan. It seems Flanagans are bringing out a new kind of whiskey called Hair of the Dog (a stupid name if you ask me), and they were to give the Boss money to have a picture of me on the label. There was to be a big party for it in Galway, called a launching. I thought that was boats; wrong again.

The Missis loves a party, and she bought a long

black dress. 'You should get a dinner suit, Jack,' says she. 'They're to be had for hiring.'

'You want to make a laughing stock of me,' says the Boss, and he put on his grey suit and his blue pullover. I thought he looked the finest, but the Missis wasn't satisfied at all.

She was fussing around telling the Boss not to drink too much. 'I'm not driving home,' says she – she has driving given up, 'and mind and call me Kathleen or I'll kill you.'

The Boss

'All right, so,' says the Boss. As a rule, he calls her Mam, but her registered name is Kathleen. Mam is her working name.

It must have been the kind of launching I know

about, because I heard you could swim in the whiskey – ugh! I stayed at home with Jess who has the pledge taken. 'It's all right for the Boss,' says she. 'It's innocent bitches and puppies that suffer.'

'Nobody suffers here except the Missis,' says I.

The Boss came home late, singing a song:

'The whiskey that's brewed by Tim Flanagan,
Drink it all up, be a man again.
Fill up as fast as you can again,
Began again . . .'

He was at it for a long time. It's very unfair that we aren't allowed to sing at night. Then he noticed me and he says, 'You have a new name, Shep, but I'm damned if I'll use it. Flanagan's Flockmaster. Beat that.'

Flanagan's Flockmaster! *Me!* The cheek of them.

It seems that the society we all belong to won't let us be sponsored, so I was back to Shep for the National Trial. There's a greyhound on the whiskey labels and the Boss was raging mad. Anyway, he's forgotten about it now, because he got on to the Irish team with me, and that was his heart's desire. To get on the team, we had to be in the first twelve in the Irish National, up in Donegal.

The Boss got a lift with Jim Dolan, whose dog Ben was running too. Jim is a big heavy man with a beard, who likes a pint and likes a song. He has his own group, which is called Irish Stew, and he drove a stationary wagon with a glass back to it, so we could see out.

Ben and me had a fine time watching other dogs

having to walk and listening to Jim and the Boss arguing. 'The best sheep for trials is Suffolks,' says the Boss.

'Cheviots is better, or Scotch Hornies,' says Jim.

'They are not,' says the Boss, 'they're useless. Texels now, they're a bit stubborn.'

'The Mountainy sheep is way the best,' says Jim.

'They might be, if you have a weak dog,' says the Boss. Before long, they got very angry altogether. They shouted away, and Jim was driving like a bat out of hell.

'Heavy sheep is no good, unless for a slow old dog,' says he.

'There's no need to shout,' says the Boss, 'I have me hearing, thanks be to God.' We went round a corner so quick, Ben let a yelp out of him, and Jim twisted round to tell him to be quiet. He made a mistake, looking round like that. There was an old bend in the road, and the car ran into a big bank. By the grace of God, the two of them had seat belts on them, or they'd have been killed stone dead. Ben and me had no seat belts; I landed on the Boss's lap, and Ben landed on Jim's.

We were all so shook, we just sat there. In a few minutes, who should come along only Mr O'Brien with his car and his little trailer. So we left the stationary wagon after us and went with him.

They used Mountainy sheep at the trial, and Jim and Ben made no hand of them. Me and the Boss would have been happier with heavy sheep, we didn't expect to win anything. But it was something like the time when the Boss had trouble with his teeth and couldn't whistle. I won that time, because he let me alone. This time it was shock that kept him quiet, and things went well for us. We were fifth, and got on the team.

There was a second day and we stayed over. The Boss and Jim met friends and missed Mr O'Brien when he was going home. One way and another, we didn't land back until Sunday. Jim's car was gone from the ditch. He left it because he thought it wouldn't go, but it did. It was taken, and the Guards got it in Waterford, in bits.

We had to go home by bus, and Ben was sick. It's the diesel goes against him, he says. The Boss said that underbred dogs were often bad travellers, and after that, him and Jim sat at opposite ends of the bus. They didn't talk since.

The International Trial is in Wales in September. The Boss and the Missis is coming, and all Coolcoffin in a coach. 'Shep and me will uphold the honour of Ireland,' says the Boss. I hope I don't let him down.

SIXTEEN

THE International Sheepdog Trial has been and gone, and I thought we'd win it, I really did. The disappointment is terrible.

It's funny about people – as far as I know, they aren't able to see ghosts. I never saw the ghost of a man until I went to Wales, but I saw the ghosts of plenty of dogs in my time. They do no harm. I wouldn't have thought sheep could see ghosts, but I know now that they can.

A whole crowd of us went to Wales. I'm used to travelling now and there wasn't a bother on me. The Boss was telling everyone we'd win, but they didn't pay any heed to him. The trial went on for three days and I had to run on the first. This was qualifying for the final on the third day. There was a dresser-load of prizes for the winner, and the Boss was wondering how he'd manage in the Customs when our number was called.

There were five sheep and I set off to fetch them as cool as you like. I never felt better, and I knew I was doing great. I had the best outrun of the day, I heard. I used to think an outrun was what the cat did when the Missis caught him in the kitchen – live and learn. It was my day; the further I went, the better I went, until I came to the pen. In the big trials, the pen isn't the end, you have to single out a sheep with a red collar after. I wasn't worrying about that.

The Boss was mesmerised by the way things were going. I thought he was going to stay standing in the shedding ring and forget to open the gate of the pen, but at the last minute he came panting up to the gate. There was six feet of rope on the gate and he had to hold it. I had the sheep lined up, just right, and they were just going in when they all stopped up in a slap.

I couldn't see why they'd stopped and I kept pushing them until I knew they'd break away if I went on, so I waited for the Boss to say something. He did. 'Go on, you idle villain – get up outa that!' was what he said. So I went on and the sheep bolted all ways and I had to bring them back. As I got them lined up again, I saw what was wrong. There was a black and white dog with one eye sitting in the pen.

'What are you doing there?' says I.

'Sitting down, amusing meself,' says he. He was from Scotland by his brogue.

'Well, get out,' says I. 'You're spoiling my boss's run.' The dog didn't move, and I noticed I could see the bars of the pen through him.

'I was called Roy,' says he. 'I won three Internationals when your Boss was a pup. It's fifty years to the minute since I won me last, so I thought I'd put in an appearance.'

'You can disappear again as soon as you like,' says I, for I knew I couldn't fight him. Then it was given out that we'd run out of time and the dog faded away. As the Boss stamped off the field with me, I heard a whistle and I saw the one-eyed dog going off with a thin man in a cap.

'The devil was in those sheep,' says Jim Dolan to the Boss when we got back.

'By the way they were acting, you'd think the devil was in the pen,' says the Boss. Aren't people unfortunate to be so blind?

❁

The Boss was so mad, he couldn't face going home with the crowd after the trial. Martin was laughing at him and the Missis cried. He had a few drinks with Jim Dolan and they decided they'd stay over and buy two dogs. There's a notion that the further you go to buy a dog the better he'll be. This isn't always right.

The International was worse for the Boss than for me. A Scottish dog told me that I'd seen the ghosts of J. M. Wilson and Roy who were the best ever and I should feel honoured, so I tried to see it his way.

We watched the final and then the others went home while we stayed on. Jim Dolan wasn't running Ben; he brought him because he'd nobody to mind him at home. He howls night and day when he is left, and sometimes he bites people when he forgets. Jim has a sister and he thinks she should take care of Ben, but she won't.

The stationary wagon was smashed up and Jim couldn't afford another, so he has a small little red Mini, but he still drives like the wheels of hell. We were to go home on the Monday afternoon on the Holyhead boat, so we had all Sunday and half Monday. The Boss had met a man called Cymro at the trial, who knew a farmer with a whole pile of dogs to sell. 'He doesn't know the value of them,' says Cymro.

We drove a long way to see them. 'What's the name of this place?' says the Boss.

'Ysgol,' says Jim. 'Look at it on that sign.'

'G'way,' says the Boss. 'We came through Ysgol miles back, I noticed the name. Funny old names they have in Wales – nothing simple like Coolcoffin.'

'Are you sure about Ysgol?' says Jim.

'Of course I'm sure. You're driving round in rings,' says the Boss.

Jim stopped so sudden that Ben and me was nearly thrown out of the back seat, and we drove back the way we came at seventy miles an hour. We stopped at the last town we'd come through and Jim pointed to a sign. 'Ysgol. Look, will you?' says he.

'Is all the towns in Wales called Ysgol?' says the Boss to a little lad who was walking up the road . . . 'He says it's Welsh for a school. Whip her round, Jim. We were right before.'

Jim whipped her round and back we went. After another hour we found the farm on a hillside. The farmer had a pile of dogs all right. There were over twenty, barking and running around. We stayed in the car while Jim and the Boss went to see them work; it was a long time before they came back. Then they all went into the house and stayed until dark.

A long time later, Jim came out, because Ben was howling. He had drink taken and the Boss had a small sup too. They put us in a stable and we were fed, but Ben was feeling sick, so I ate his food. The Welsh dogs barked all night, and we could hear the Boss singing 'Spancilhill' in the house. Ben howled like a banshee and I slept badly.

I thought I was still having nightmares next day. Jim and the Boss had bought four dogs.

CHAPTER SEVENTEEN

I was glad to hear that the dogs were all for Jim and a friend of his.

It was a tight fit in the Mini; I sat in front at the Boss's feet and the other five were in the back. The nearest dog to me was big and black. 'I'll introduce us,' says he. 'This is Taff, those two are Gwen and Meg. You may call me Bach.'

'Bark?' says I. 'I heard you last night.'

'Not Bark, Bach,' says the dog. 'I suppose you're Pat or Mick.'

'I'm Shep,' says I. 'I won on the telly.'

Bark

'I remember now,' says Bark. 'I thought Ifor Jenkins was in terrible hard luck.'

'I don't know about hard luck,' says I. His dog didn't take his commands at the pen.

'How do you know?' growled Bark, 'Do you know Welsh?'

'I know you can't whistle in Welsh,' says I.

'Ah, shut up,' says Bark. 'Your Boss was drunk, anyway.' There's limits to what I can stand, so I squithered through beside the seat and grabbed him by the neck. Taff came to help Bark; there was no room at all.

'Help me, Ben,' says I, with me mouth full of Welsh wool.

'I can't,' says Ben, 'I'm going to be sick,' and he was. Gwen and Meg, who weren't used to driving, were sick as well. They'd had meat dinners and milk.

'Stop, can't you,' roars the Boss. 'Jim, stop the car.'

'I can't,' says Jim, 'we'll miss the boat.' All the time, he'd been flying down the narrow roads like a bullet.

The Boss opened his seat belt and twisted around. He knelt on the seat and beat us all with a rolled-up newspaper. It didn't hurt. 'For God's sake stop,' says he. 'The Welsh Guards is after us.'

'They have policemen over here, not guards,' says Jim, with his foot on the pedal. 'They won't touch us because we're tourists.'

'I wouldn't bank on it,' says the Boss. 'They're passing us out.'

I was still underneath Taff and Bark, so I couldn't see what happened. I felt the car stop with a jolt, and all six of us fell in a heap with me at the bottom of it. I heard a voice say, 'Do you realise you were travelling at seventy-seven miles an hour?'

'Is that so?' says Jim. 'Your roads are so good, you wouldn't feel the speed creeping up on you.

'I'll have to report you.'

'Let us go, we'll miss the boat to Ireland,' says Jim.

'Who owns all the dogs?' says the voice.

'He does,' says Jim and the Boss together.

'You aren't wearing your seatbelt,' says the voice to the Boss.

'Have sense, man,' says the Boss. 'Would you, if there was three dogs fighting behind you and three getting sick?'

'You'll be hearing from us,' says the voice.

Soon we were off again, as fast as ever, and never stopped until we reached a river with a notice, PRIVATE: NO BATHING. Jim and the Boss took each of us in turn and washed us in the river – I was last out. 'Did you ever get washed before, since your Mammy cleaned you?' says Bark, and I had to attack him again.

Taff joined in, and Ben, who was feeling better. Jim came to separate us and slipped, and me and him and Bark all fell in the river, so Jim got a wash as well.

A few carloads of people drove by, and they were all watching us. You'd think they never saw a dog-fight before. Gwen got loose and was nearly run over. It was an hour before we were back on the road again.

❂

After we'd got washed, Jim drove faster than ever. We flew down the roads with the wheels bouncing on the bumps and I was sure we'd be over the ditch. We went through Holyhead as if we were going to a

69

fire, and when we reached the harbour, there was the boat, the width of a small field out from the side, steaming away to Dublin without us. I did truly think Jim was going to drive into the sea after it. He stopped just in time, and him and the Boss had a right row.

They asked when was the next boat, and were told it had gone, but there was one out of Fishguard in three hours. 'Fishguard? Where's that?' says the Boss.

'It's to the south,' says Jim. Down went the foot on the pedal, and we set off for Fishguard. By then, me and Taff was feeling sick and Ben, Gwen and Meg thought they were dying. It seems it's further to Fishguard than Jim thought and he lost his way twice. As well as that, we were stopped by the same police as before and they took Jim's name. It was the same old story; we landed into Fishguard as the boat sailed away.

'That's it,' says the Boss, 'I'll travel no farther with you, I'd sooner walk.' Him and me got out of the car, but Jim begged him to go on to a place called Pembroke where he'd get another ferry.

'How in hell am I to keep five dogs out of the front seat if you aren't there?' says he.

The Boss said yes, he supposed it might be a bit dangerous, so we got in again and were soon on the road to Pembroke. It was dark by then and a hard road to find, so Jim eased up a little and none of us was sick.

Pembroke at three in the morning isn't a great spot. I suppose it isn't fair to judge it – a Welsh dog might say the same of Coolcoffin at three in the morning. We had five hours to wait. We all slept in the car and it was nice and warm, but you'd call it smelly if you were fussy. Jim and the Boss were snoring away when it was time for the boat to go, so it was a good job somebody woke them up.

Soon we were on the boat and Jim says, 'Well, Jack, we're clear of Wales at last. We're off in five minutes. Next stop Dublin.' Just then, along came two policemen and asked for Jim by name.

'You've been reported,' says they. 'Overcrowding a car, beating six dogs while travelling at an excessive speed, no seatbelts, attempting to drown two dogs, bathing in a private place and allowing a dog to stray on to the public highway.'

'It's your car. You go,' says the Boss.

So Jim went off with the policemen and the boat was delayed an hour and a half while they asked him questions. I don't know what happened, as me and Ben stayed with the Boss, and the other dogs were in the car. The policemen seemed quite happy when they came back. One of them shook the Boss by the hand and the other patted Ben's head. By the grace of God he didn't forget himself and bite him – he's handy with his teeth and he was feeling sick.

There was a big gale on the way back to Ireland. We all thought we were going to Dublin, but no, it was Wexford, where we went before, by mistake. Jim was desperate to get home and wouldn't delay a minute, so we set off at once on the long road, right across Ireland.

Now he's home, the Boss says he'll never travel abroad again, not for a thousand Internationals.

EIGHTEEN

WELL, another winter has gone, and St Patrick's Day has come round again. The parade in Coolcoffin isn't as big as the one in Dublin, but it's better, I dare say. This year, me and the Boss was asked to be in it, marching behind the pipe band. Me and Jess could hear the band practising from the farm and we joined in because it pained our ears; I didn't want to march behind it at all. The Boss was looking forward to it.

When the day came, the Boss slipped in the yard and twisted his ankle, so he said he wouldn't be able to march and he'd have to ride on one of the floats. Martin drove us down to where everyone was collecting, but nobody wanted us on their trailer.

The travel agent is the Boss's second cousin, so he had to say yes. He had a fine trailer with palm trees and girls in bikinis. He brought a chair out of the kitchen for the Boss to sit on and hoisted him up. I hopped up beside him. 'Will you take that raincoat off you, Jack,' says the travel agent. 'You're spoiling me image.'

'I will not,' says the Boss.

We rode through the town in fine style; I was very proud. There was a small crowd because nearly everybody was in the procession. We saw two Americans taking photos of us, and when it was over, they got talking to the Boss. They were real friendly and full of old chat. 'Would you like to be in a movie?' says one of them.

'I would so,' says the Boss. 'I like a good cowboy.'

'This isn't a cowboy, it's a historical picture,' says the American. 'We want an old shepherd for atmosphere. You'd only have a couple of lines to say, but you'd need to grow a beard.'

'I'm not growing any beard,' says the Boss.

'Never mind, then. If you can't grow one, we'll ask Mr Denis O'Brien or Mr Jim Dolan. They could grow beards.'

'Who says I couldn't?' says the Boss. 'I could grow one down to me knees if I wanted to.'

For the next few weeks he looked a fright, all grey fuzz, growing sideways, not downwards. The Missis had a job to keep from laughing, but he said it was all in a good cause. He learned his lines in no time. 'Lie down Bob,' was one (I was Bob), and 'It looks like snow,' was the other.

My part was much harder; I had to howl on his grave. I couldn't make out what they wanted me to do until they got the idea of having the Coolcoffin pipe band playing behind the hedge.

Coolcoffin is a sad place now. We were looking forward to being film stars, and the Missis had it all made up that we were going on a cruise. I don't mind missing that – I'd enough cruising coming back from Wales. The Boss got a letter saying we weren't wanted because they'd found a shepherd with a bigger beard and a dog which would howl without an orchestra to accompany him. That wasn't fair. The pipe band wouldn't help, so Martin was going to play a few screeches on his fiddle. That would put me howling for ten minutes.

The Boss took it so hard, the two Americans called to tell him they'd let him know if there was another part for him. 'Who's this actor you've found?' says the Boss.

'Mr Jim Dolan,' says they. 'His dog is called Ben.' After that, the Missis made tea while the Boss attacked his beard. She let him get over it and said nothing. She manages him better since she got liberated.

This liberation was a great thing. I never knew the Missis to be tied up, so I wondered what it meant. She told the Boss about it and he said it was codology, but she went to a meeting in spite of him and came back liberated. I couldn't see any difference, but some of the women went mad altogether, joining the hurling team and burning their vests. I think that's what the Missis said.

As for the picture, there was to be a crowd scene, but the Boss wouldn't be in it, not when he'd nearly been a shepherd for atmosphere. He kept out of the way, and made Martin help him shear the sheep. He was clipping away with the electric machine when the two Americans turned up with cameras.

'Shearing time,' says they. 'What luck. Could you shear a sheep by hand? We'll put it in the picture.'

The Boss was sorry his beard was gone. He caught a sheep and started snipping away with the hand shears Martin was using for clipping the dirty bits off the fleeces. The shears were blunt and it wasn't a thing he'd ever tried before. I was more than sorry for that sheep – he didn't cut her often or deeply, but he was as slow as he could be. When she was half done, she got away and Martin fell over me as we both tried to stop her. There was wool trailing all over and she wasn't going to be caught again if she could help it.

Round and round the shed we went, and at last me and Martin and the Boss all dived at the sheep at once. She gave a big lep and landed on top of the camera; her legs got tangled in some wires and she and the two men rolled about on the ground.

I thought it was very funny, but then I'm not educated or anything.

We are not going to be in the picture after all. The Boss is taking the Missis to Lisdoonvarna for the weekend to make up for it.

NINETEEN

LISDOONVARNA is where the Boss met the Missis first. Ever since, the two of them has taken a holiday there in September but they missed last year because of going to Wales. The Missis was highly delighted to be going.

Martin and me was left to mind the farm. Tiny is sold at last, to Mr O'Brien, and Jess is expecting again, but I draw the line at working for Martin, so he had to get the cows on his own.

Martin was eating his dinner on the Friday and I was lying on the doorstep when I heard a car tearing down the road; then I heard brakes and tyres squealing. Jim Dolan in his Mini came racing into our yard and flattened one hen. In the back of the car sat Ben, Taff and Bark.

Martin came out and peeled the hen off the cement. 'She'll make soup,' says Jim. 'Here, I heard your mam and dad is gone to Lisdoon. I'd the notion of going meself – I might meet a nice girl like your dad did.'

'They're gone since morning,' says Martin. 'You've missed them.'

'I'll be there as soon as them,' says Jim, 'this is a great little car. Look, Martin, will you be a good lad and mind these dogs till Monday? You won't know you have them.'

'I have dogs enough to mind,' says Martin. 'I have three, and Ben bites people.'

'Not like he did,' says Jim. 'Not as hard nor as often.'

'I don't care,' says Martin, 'I won't have him.'

'All right so,' says Jim, 'I'll take him with me. You can keep Taff and Bark – they're millers to work.' Martin said nothing. He took Taff and Bark to the pony's stable and shut them in. 'Good man, I'm grateful to you,' says Jim, getting into the car. 'If anyone comes along with £300 in his pocket you can sell him Bark. He is a little bit hasty with sheep.' With that, gravel flew all over as he raced out of the yard.

Taff is a harmless enough dog, a middling good worker and no trouble on his own. It's Bark is the bad influence. He looked bigger and blacker than ever, his ears stand out sideways from his head and he has wild, yellow eyes. I once heard Jim say he never let him off the chain except to work, and I soon found out why. The bottom of the stable door was mended to keep Tiny in, not so long ago. It is new timber but, before me very eyes, Bark tore it asunder. He pulled out half inch boards with three inch nails in them, and he was out in a couple of minutes with Taff after him.

I says to Bark, 'Now look what you're after doing. Your Boss will have to pay for a new door.'

'He'll do no such thing,' says Bark. 'That door was rotten, ready to fall to bits. Now. Where do you keep your sheep? The trouble with Ireland is there's nothing to do.'

'The sheep are sold,' says I. (That was a lie; may I

be forgiven.) 'If you want a job, why don't you bring the bullocks up from the bog?' That'll beat him, I thought, and I went back to the step. Taff, who doesn't like cattle, came with me.

Five minutes later, all twenty bullocks ran bawling through the yard with Bark snapping at their heels. They broke the gate and galloped into the vegetable garden. Me and Taff went under the henhouse. We wished the Boss was home.

❀

The Missis grows all kinds of things in the garden – cabbages and carrots and onions. She has flowers too, but I don't know what they're for. She cuts them like cabbages and brings them in; then after a few days she throws them out again without using them for anything.

When Martin heard Bark and the bullocks in the garden, he didn't know what to do. I had to help him out of pity. We drove the cattle into the small yard by the road, and Martin grabbed Bark's collar as he went by and slammed the gate. All the time, a small man was leaning on the wall, watching him.

Now I knew it was Chris, the man who wanted to buy Tiny at the dog sale, but Martin wasn't with us that day. 'That black dog is good after cattle,' says he. 'Is he for sale?'

'He is,' says Martin, 'but the price is £400.' Martin isn't clever like the Boss, and he saw his chance to earn praise.

'I'll buy,' says Chris, 'if I get £50 back for luck.' He wrote out a cheque for £400 then and there.

'You should have stopped the luck money out of it,' says Martin.

'Never do that,' says Chris, 'it helps the taxman.'
Martin went inside and brought out five ten pound
notes. Chris took Bark and the money and drove
away.

Martin was in great humour for the rest of the
weekend. The bank was shut till Monday, but he
meant to get the money all in tenners, so Jim would
give him one for very shame. On Saturday, he went
to Coolcoffin and bought a box of chocolates for
Julia, his girl-friend. In the evening, she came to the
farm and they ate them. On Sunday, he went to a
match. Sunday night late, the Boss and the Missis
came home after Martin was gone to bed. I was
never more pleased to see anyone.

In the morning, I heard the Boss and Martin talking. 'How could I tell the cheque was no good?' says
Martin.

'Your own common sense should have told you.
The chequebook was taken out of somebody's
pocket at the races. What did your man look like?'

'He was a small man in a cap,' says Martin.

'Where was he from?'

'He didn't say.'

'Where was he going?'

'I didn't ask him.'

'What kind of car had he?' The Boss was getting
angrier by the minute.

'It was cream or white – or maybe silver,' says
Martin. 'A Ford, I think, or a Toyota. Oldish. I didn't
notice the number.'

Out comes the Missis then, in a right state. 'There's
£50 gone out of the dresser,' says she. So then Martin
had to explain about the luckpenny. By the time the
Boss was finished with him, I was real sorry for him.

And then Jim arrived in a van he'd got a loan of because a tree had collided with his Mini on the Lisdoonvarna road. He wasn't as mad as the Boss, because he had a dislike taken to Bark, and he had to admit he forced Martin into minding him. He said he wanted no payment; he'd take a pup sometime.

I don't think we've seen the last of Bark. He likes to be noticed and he must be the noisiest dog in Ireland.

TWENTY

SOMETIMES the Boss goes over to Mr O'Brien's place for a day gathering sheep on the hills. There's thousands of them up there, and he gets money for taking me and helping to move them. I little thought where I'd end up when we set off last time.

The first man I saw on the mountain was Chris, who paid for Bark with a bad cheque. He had a white collie with him – at least she was meant to be white. She told me her name was Floosie. 'What's your name?' says she.

'I'm Shep,' says I proudly, 'I won on the telly.'

'Oh, you do the telly ads for the worm dose, don't you?' says she. ' "No parasites now," says Shep, "thanks to Vermolin." ' I was ashamed. I said nothing.

'Don't mind me,' says Floosie, 'I'm only a sheep-killer, even if I am well connected. I wish I'd had your chances, so I do.'

'A sheep-killer?' says I. 'That's murder. You get shot for it.'

'I know that,' says Floosie cheerfully, 'and I'm such a good target too, all white. Don't look so horrified – I've helped to kill dozens of sheep, rounding them up for the gang near Dublin.'

We had to start work then, and I found it hard to mind my job, watching her. Most of us are related and I didn't want to admit to being cousin to a murderess, so when I got the chance, I asked her, 'Do you have Papers?'

'I do,' snarled Floosie. '113765, thank you very much, Ballybog Drift, sold as a pup and reared in a high-rise flat. Now are you satisfied? And I don't fetch the hens in for the Missis and I'm not let have any pups neither. Now shut your gob; you give me a pain.' She turned her back and began looking for fleas.

Floosie

We worked all morning, and Floosie had more style than all the other dogs put together. I says to her, 'It's in the trials you should be.'

'I wouldn't bother me head,' says Floosie. 'I'm a better worker than Finn there, even if he did come second at Ballyjamesduff the year before last. Go home to the Missis and sit by the fire – you might get a rasher for your tea. Tiny's a better dog than you; if he'd been with the gang we'd never have gone hungry.'

I wondered what was annoying her but I didn't dare ask. As for Tiny, he'd just pulled a big lump of wool out of a sheep. I decided to keep quiet.

I rode home in the front of the car with the Boss for the first time that evening. He'd enjoyed the day and was singing 'Spancilhill', but I was tired and I kept thinking about Floosie. I told Jess about her when I got home. 'I know her sort,' says Jess, 'she's a white slave, that's what she is.'

❊

A couple of days after that, everyone was away at a Field Evening in Coolcoffin. I was minding the house and Jess was shut up. A white car stopped at our gate and that Chris got out and lifted up the boot lid. I thought he was bringing Bark home, so I went to see, and there was Floosie's dirty white face looking out. 'Hello, Handsome,' says she. She'd got over her temper.

'How are you going on?' says I, and I jumped in beside her for a chat.

'You're a right eejit, Shep,' says Floosie.

'Why?' says I. The boot lid banged shut.

'That's the why,' says Floosie. The car started and drove away.

I scratched and yelped, and Floosie says, 'Be quiet, will you? Do you want to bring my Boss round to us?'

'Is he cruel? Does he beat you?' I wanted to know.

'No,' says Floosie, 'he's too good a handler for that, but he'd beat us if it'd make us work better. He's hard. No heart.'

'Why do you work for him, so?' says I.

'Because I'm a dog, of course. Stop asking stupid questions and go to sleep.' Floosie went to sleep herself, but I didn't.

At last we stopped, and Chris opened the boot. We were in a locked yard. Chris tied Floosie up in a shed where there was another dog on a chain, then he threw three dead rabbits into the shed. He waited for me to go in but I wasn't hungry. I was thinking of my people coming home and missing me. Then Chris tried to catch me, but I backed off and stripped me teeth.

'I'd advise you to eat that rabbit,' says Floosie. 'We don't get fancy dogfood here. Even your black friend got hungry after a while, the noisy brute. If Snap here doesn't catch any rabbits, we're lucky if we're fed every day.' I looked at Snap. You could call him a sheepdog if you were shortsighted, but his legs were twice as long as mine.

'I'm unique,' says Snap, 'if you know what that means. One of my grandfathers won the International and the other won the Greyhound Derby.' I was going to say I won on the telly, then I thought I'd better not.

Floosie started on her rabbit. 'You can have a bit of this if you like, Lover Boy,' says she, 'I'm saving the best bits for you.' She sounded as if she meant it. I went into the shed and Chris shut the door. 'You soft old fool,' says Floosie, 'caught twice by the same trick. You've spent too long under the kitchen table, no wonder they codded you into selling worm pills.' She turned on me, showing every tooth in her head. 'Leave that rabbit alone if you want to stay in one piece. Eat your own.'

I was ashamed. I said nothing.

TWENTY-ONE

I was pure, solid miserable at Chris's place. He took me out on the hill with Floosie, and I have to confess I worked for him – my best – and I helped him to steal sheep. 'Ah, you can't help yourself, you're a dog, like I said,' says Floosie.

I didn't know what to make of Floosie. When she put her head down on her paws and peeped up at me sideways, she'd have charmed the heart out of a cabbage, but I could never keep up with her moods. Sometimes she called me Lover Boy or Dreamy Eyes; other times it was Softy or Flatfeet and she'd bite as soon as look at you. I still don't understand one bit of her, so I don't. As for Snap, he just laughed at me and I wouldn't have eaten the rabbits he caught if we'd got anything else.

Chris took me and Floosie up on the hill every evening about dusk. He'd keep me on a chain until I could see the sheep, then he'd let me go and I'd work for him. He had a squeaky voice and he smelled of beer and cabbage and mice, but he understood dogs. Floosie said he could even make Bark behave but he had to give him to a friend because he was too noisy for stealing.

My trouble is, I'm not a one-man dog. I work for

the Boss, the Missis, Mr O'Brien – anyone who can handle a dog. I worked for that squint-eyed black-guard, just like Floosie said I would, and he even taught me a new command. When he wanted me to fetch the sheep, he whistled like a curlew. I soon learned.

One night it was late, and as black as the hob of hell. We waited in a lonesome place for the moon to rise, then we rounded up a dozen sheep and drove them into a trailer. I nearly died when Floosie told me we were stealing them, although I knew I'd help Chris to steal more if he asked me. It's a dog's life, being a dog.

One day when we were locked up as usual, I heard Mr O'Brien talking to Chris. He said, 'Jack Kelly has lost Shep. I wondered –' I heard no more because Floosie and Snap began to bark as loud as they were able. I barked too, but it's a thing I never do, my voice wouldn't have been known. The others never stopped until Mr O'Brien's car was gone.

'We don't want to lose you, Softy,' says Floosie.

The man who owned the trailer was called Joe. Him and Chris were planning to take a whole lorry-load of sheep off the hills. Chris was sure Mr O'Brien had guessed I was there and why; he was afraid to go on with the job. Chris and Joe were ages arguing in the yard, but Joe got his way in the end.

That night, I sang the saddest song I knew, 'The Kerry Blues'.

'Shut your mouth, will you,' says Floosie, 'or you'll get us all beaten. I heard Joe say your Boss was offering a big reward for you – think of that now! I was dumped out of a car, fifty miles from home by my own boss. I was lucky Chris picked me up. Count your blessings, Softy,' says she.

❀

When the time came, Chris took me and Floosie up the hill in his car and we met Joe. Then we walked a nice bit, to the edge of the Forestry, where the lorry was waiting. It was black dark near the trees, but in the open we could see sheep scattered all over. Me and Floosie went around them, one each side, then Chris gave his curlew whistle and we fetched them to the lorry. Now we dogs knew quite well that there were other people about, in among the trees, but that wasn't our business. We loaded the sheep – more than a hundred of them, and nothing happened until Chris and Joe were putting up the back of the lorry. Then suddenly there was guards everywhere. They grabbed Chris and Joe and I saw that Mr O'Brien was with them.

'Which dog was stolen?' says one of the guards, 'Can you prove it?'

'I can,' says Mr O'Brien, and he told me to go in on the sheeps' backs and fetch them out of the lorry. So I did that and then I jumped up at him, which I am not allowed to do, but I forgot meself.

'That's proof enough,' says the Guard, 'You can return him to Mr Kelly.'

'Are you coming, Floosie?' says I.

'Not me,' says Floosie. 'I'll stick by this villain here. See you in prison, Softy,' says she. Mr O'Brien took me back to his own place and next morning early, he took me home to Coolcoffin.

We turned into the yard and there was the Missis and she says, 'Oh, Denis, indeed we're grateful for all your trouble, but I know in my own mind poor Shep is dead.' Then she saw me in the car, and I'll skip the next bit because I was embarrassed. I mean, I think the world an' all of the Missis, but wasn't I glad Floosie hadn't come along! I was so happy, I raced three times round our yard, jumping at the swallows like poor Dolly used to do (she never caught one either). The Missis thought all I went through must have turned me brain.

Next, out came the Boss. He was only after getting up. 'There's a reward for you, Denis,' says he, 'Get down, will you, you old fool, it's worth £100 to have Shep back.' But Mr O'Brien said it was enough reward to see us together again.

'He's in a terrible mess,' says he, 'but I didn't want to delay getting him home.' So he stayed for breakfast and the Boss gave him whiskey and the Missis gave him tea and scrambled eggs, and he said he never had such a breakfast in his life.

I had a bath and a big plate of 'Collywobbles'. There was such excitement that Martin went to the creamery without the milk and had to come back for it. Everybody talked, one against the other, and Jamesy Quinn came round and Mrs Quinn and some of the other neighbours.

I sat under the kitchen table and scratched and scratched. They have a terrible breed of flea where I was staying.

TWENTY-TWO

I used to think Coolcoffin was the finest town in Ireland, but now I know it isn't. Galway City is. The Boss was there lately at a meeting, trying to get the Government to do something – I forget what. They're not going to do it anyway.

The Missis came to buy a dress to wear at Martin's wedding and I went along for the ride – they hardly let me out of their sight now. After she'd looked at a lot of dresses, the Missis took me to a place called 'The Dog Shop', to buy me a new collar with a nameplate on it. It was a new shop and she got a great surprise when she found out that the owner was Miss Cairngorm, who stayed with us two Christmasses ago.

Miss Cairngorm was delighted to meet the Missis again. 'I know you must be dying to see my precious Teazie again,' says she, and she calls him into the shop. It was easy to see that Mr Teazie-Weazie wasn't dying to see me again. 'I've got another dog now,' says Miss Cairngorm. 'Poor thing, I picked her up straying on the road, miles from anywhere. She's a pretty creature, but doesn't agree with my gorgeous boy.' (She meant Teazie-Weazie! Could you believe it?)

She went to the door and called, 'Here, Blanche,' and I nearly dropped when Floosie swaggered into the shop, clean and shining and wearing a tartan collar. 'Would you give her a good home?' says Miss Cairngorm.

'I don't know,' says the Missis. 'I'd have to ask the Boss.'

'Hello, Dreamy Eyes,' says Floosie to me, 'I'll come with you this time if I get the chance. Old Lassie here is driving me crackers.'

'I am *not* called Lassie,' says Mr Teazie-Weazie. 'I keep telling you, it's the breed. I was at Crufts, I'd have you know, and I should have won. There's too much corruption nowadays.'

I was puzzled. I know about corruption – it smells good and you roll in it and then they won't let you into the house. I'm not sure about Crufts, but I think they might be small farms in Scotland. 'I won on the telly,' says I.

'Really?' says Teazie, 'I don't watch the farming programmes, I'm afraid.'

Floosie lay down with her head on the Missis's foot and rolled her eyes up at her. That did it. Down went the Missis on the two knees. 'Isn't she a dote?' says she. 'I'll chance taking her now, and I'll bring her back if Jack kicks up. Will that do?' Then she took us both to the car where we waited for the Boss.

When he came, he started to give out, then he had a closer look at Floosie. 'Well, there's justice for you,' says he. 'I'll take me Bible oath that's Chris's Floosie.'

'Her name's Blanche,' says the Missis.

'Blanche, where are ye,' says the Boss. 'She's Floosie, one of the best dogs in the West. Chris is in

90

jail, so we'll keep her all right and I'll buy you a present before we go.' He sang 'Spancilhill' all the way home.

❁

Floosie and Jess don't get on at all. I was afraid of it. In fact, Jess isn't talking to me because she blames me for bringing Floosie here. When I asked Floosie why wouldn't she settle down with me and Jess and rear some pups to occupy her time, she showed all her beautiful white teeth in what might have been a smile and didn't bother to answer. 'Don't you like puppies, Floosie?' says I.

'Love 'em,' says Floosie. 'I had seven half-spaniels once. They died young, poor little things – I don't care to talk about it.'

'Give you half a chance and you'll be sheep-worrying again,' says Jess.

'I will not,' says Floosie. I'm anti blood-sports now. I'll be going when they let Chris out of prison, though. I don't like your Boss – he knows more about a plate of bacon and cabbage than he does about a sheepdog. Besides, he sings out of tune.'

❁

Martin and Julia are married at last. Martin kept putting it off for one reason and another, but once the Missis had her new dress she told him to get on with it and they were married last Saturday. They're building a new house down the road, and they're going there as soon as it's finished.

The wedding was great gas. Martin wouldn't buy a suit, but the Missis said he couldn't get married in jeans or a tracksuit. Martin didn't see why not, but he borrowed a suit from his cousin Dan. Him and Dan isn't the same size, but even so.

I didn't get taken to the church, but I did go to the reception in a big hotel in Galway. The wedding party was a bit like the dinner I was at in England, but noisier, and there was a dance after it. The Boss sang his new song, 'Lanigan's Ball', which is about Julia, and he danced with Julia until Martin got fed up and went off to the bar.

The party went on till night. I got a plate of chicken and ham and then I went to sleep. When I woke, everyone was gone, so I went to the door and saw Martin and Julia driving away in our car. I thought I was being left behind and I didn't see the Boss in the crowd, so I ran out into the street after the car. I missed getting run over by a whisker. Me blood runs cold when I think of it. The Boss was there all the time – he had drink taken and forgot about me.

He came straight after me, in among all the cars, and I saw him and went to him. Some of the cars ran into each other and there was breaking glass and bad language, but we didn't pay any heed. We went back into the hotel together and left them to sort themselves out. Somebody gave me some stout to drink; I don't think it's all it's cracked up to be.

I don't remember coming home.

TWENTY-THREE

IT's a while since I wrote anything. For one thing, there's been a lot of fighting going on here, which I don't like at all. Julia doesn't get on with the Missis, and Floosie doesn't get on with Jess. To make it worse, Jess takes it out on me. She says it isn't natural for dogs to write books, but I say, if Birds can make custard, dogs can write books. Then she says me grammar is bad!

When I said that I lived with the Boss, the Missis, Jess, who is black with a chaney eye, and Floosie,

Jess is black with a chaney eye

93

she said it sounded as if the Missis was called Jess and was black with a chaney eye. This is wrong, of course. The Missis is pink, with grey hair and blue eyes and she is called Kathleen. Jess is black, with a chaney eye and a black nose with two pink spots on it.

However, Floosie will always back me up, just to annoy Jess, so I'll start again. Martin and Julia have a baby now, and they've moved into their new house. Floosie and Jess had a big fight one night, and they both bit me when I tried to stop it, so now Floosie's gone to live with Martin and Julia, and life is duller.

The latest bit of excitement is the Boss's brother coming to stay. In Coolcoffin, nearly everybody has a sister or brother in the States. It is what's called a States symbol. The Boss has a brother in New York.

I asked a dog which has travelled a lot, 'What's New York like?'

'I don't know,' says he. 'It was York I went to for the International. I suppose New York is the same only newer.'

One day, the Boss got a letter from the brother, saying he was coming on a visit. He is called Yank – funny name. The Boss read the letter aloud to the Missis. 'He says he's bringing money for Martin,' says he. 'A big lot of dollars on account of not being at the wedding. He's flying to Shannon, and we're to meet him at seventeen hours.'

'The harmless man,' says the Missis, 'there's only twelve hours in the day.'

'It's different in America,' says the Boss.

Martin came to the farm on Sunday with Julia and the baby. The Missis was saying how big he is, but I was disgusted and so was Jess. His eyes are open already, but he can't move around at all. He looks a little bit like the Boss, but maybe he'll alter.

The day before Yank was to arrive, we had a telegram. The Missis says a telegram is always bad news, so she wouldn't open it until the Boss came home. 'Is it bad news, Jack?' says she. 'Did something happen to the brother?'

'It's the worst of news,' says the Boss, and he looked so angry I went under the kitchen table. 'Listen to this. "Please arrange sleeping quarters for bad-tempered German Shepherd." The brother must be gone clean mad.'

The Missis was raging. 'What a nerve!' says she. 'He'll have to sleep in the best room on the settee. What would a shepherd be doing in New York, anyway?'

'Why the hell doesn't he stay in New York?' says the Boss, grinding his teeth with temper. 'And suppose he has no English, what then? Who's going to talk German to him? And why's he bringing him at all if he's bad tempered? Upsetting decent, clean-living people.' He crumpled up the telegram and poked it into the range.

We all went to Shannon to meet Yank; me, the Boss, the Missis, Martin, Julia and the baby. We got the loan of a big car for the day. Yank is a small little man, half the size of the Boss and with quite a different scent. I didn't like it at first, it made me sneeze, but I'm getting used to it by degrees. He was grinning away, standing by a big pile of cases with a big, cross-looking dog on a chain.

'Where'd you get the dog?' was the first thing the Boss said to him.

'This is the German Shepherd,' says Yank. 'I have

him hired from Shannon Security as a guard for the money I brought. Answers to the name of Otto.'

'That's an Alstation,' says the Missis. 'I'm not having that sleeping on the settee in the best room.'

'Why, I should just think not,' says Yank. 'He should be locked up in a safe place at night. He's very valuable. What's up? I wired you I was bringing him.'

I went a bit nearer to Otto. 'Hello,' says I.

'*Achtung*,' says Otto, growling and showing his teeth.

'Ach what?' says I.

'*Tung*,' says Otto. '*Schweinehund*,' he says.

I was going to deal with him then and there, only the Missis grabbed me by the collar. 'Take that brute right back to the Security Boys,' says she. 'Me sister got bitten by an Alstation twenty years back and she isn't the better of it yet. The bite mortified and brought on variegated ulsters.' The Missis doesn't often put her foot down, but when she does, people do what she says without arguing – even the Boss.

Otto did not come to Coolcoffin.

TWENTY-FOUR

YOU learn something every day. I have found out that the Boss's brother wasn't registered Yank at all. His real name is Paddy. What a come-down. Being called Paddy in Coolcoffin is like being called Shep – there's too many. And Yank hasn't even got a number that I know of.

Martin's baby has been named Patrick Jeremiah after Yank. They took him to church to get him registered! The priest had to do it, they tell me. The baby's called Peejay for short so they won't get mixed up.

Yank is still here and the Missis is dead sick of him. 'He's under me feet,' says she. So him and the Boss have been going out a lot. They went three days to Galway races without coming home at all. The Missis was as cross as a bagful of cats, and to crown all, they sent word they were staying at the seaside in Salthill.

'I suppose it's bathing you were,' says the Missis when they came back, both very quiet and being careful not to get under her feet.

'Bathing, how are you?' says the Boss. 'I'm not so far gone that I'll get wet through without I have to.'

'We brought you something, Kathleen,' says Yank,

handing her a big box of chocolates.

'I'm very thankful, Paddy,' says she, 'although I don't know is it right to be eating chocolate with millions starving.'

She soon had most of them eaten – she let Yank eat the hard ones. She was saying after that, Yank was never at home. 'I never know if I should put down a dinner for him,' says she.

'Ah, there's no pleasing you,' says the Boss. 'Me own brother after all the years, spending a week or two—'

'A week or two? It's over two months! Why can't he stay with Martin – he's the one that's getting the money.' But Martin was away on a Young Farmers' tour.

At last one day, I heard the Boss saying Yank had his passage booked for a week's time. The Missis got out the handkerchief. 'We'll have a big farewell party,' says she, 'the biggest ever. Poor Paddy, the grand man, we'll miss him terrible when he goes. I declare to God he's like me own brother.'

The Boss went down to Coolcoffin to ask Jim Dolan would he and his group, Irish Stew, play for the hooley. Jim said of course they would. 'None of that old pop now,' says the Boss. Him and me went back home after calling in to fix about the drinks. That took a long time.

Yank went fishing that day, and as he came in he happened to hear the Boss shouting at me, 'G'home outa that, Shep, you useless eejit.' He doesn't mean it. 'Dog's not worth feeding,' says he, 'I'd be better off without him.'

At tea, Yank says, 'If you don't want Shep, I'll take him back to the States with me.'

The Boss said nothing, he was attacking a fry. The Missis nearly dropped the teapot. 'You can't take Shep,' says she. 'What'd we do without him? Besides, he'd be put in quarantine for six months.' I went out; I'm not going to America for anybody.

Jess got a better education than me. 'What's quarantine, do you know?' says I to her.

Jess is wonderful, the things she knows. 'It's a kind of poultice,' says she. 'It's what they put on Mrs Quinn's variegated ulsters. The doctor murdered hell out of her she said.' They seem to have some queer notions in America.

Martin wasn't back from the tour in time for the party, and the Missis was sure he met with an accident. 'The poor lad,' says she, 'and he was going to sing "The Fields of Athenry". He had it learned off special.'

Yank wasn't at an Irish hooley in thirty years. 'I can't wait to take the floor in a good set,' says he, 'the "Siege of Ennis" or the "Walls of Limerick".' They turned me out of doors along with most of the furniture. The food and drink was in the best room. I sat on the step, close up to the door – I didn't want to miss the fun.

'There'll be old-time waltzes and sets, nothing else,' says the Boss, 'I'll see to that.'

'Aren't you very square?' says the Missis.

The Boss looked down at his belly 'I'd say I was more round, like,' says he.

With all the excitement, it's a wonder the cows got milked at all that evening. They were going out to the field as Jim Dolan roared up in his red van with

'Irish Stew' on the side of it. The other players are called Mick and Ned. They unloaded a big pile of machinery with wires out of it, and began to set it up in the kitchen. 'What's all that stuff for,' says the Boss, curious, like.

'It's amplifying equipment for the vocalist,' says Jim.

'Talk sense,' says the Boss.

'It's a machine to make the singing louder,' says Jim.

The Boss began to turn red. 'Haven't you lungs?' says he. 'If you want more noise, there's as much stout and whiskey as you can drink inside in the room to put power in you.'

'Martin's coming later on,' says Jim, 'he has a smashing new song, but he needs extra volume.'

'I don't know what you're on about,' says the Boss, 'Martin's voice is plenty loud enough and I'm not going to be wired up to the lights when *I* sing.'

Soon the house was filled with people, some of them sheepdog handlers from away off. When Irish Stew began to play, they were worse than the Noise Boys from Knockcroghery. I got up in a hurry and went out to my place under the henhouse where I go when something bad is happening. Jess was there already. 'They're going mad inside,' says I. 'They sound like the Blazers at feeding time.' We lay there shivering until we heard Martin's car arriving, then we went out to meet him.

Now maybe you won't believe this, but Martin's red hair was as green as grass, and greener than most grass. He had a tag in his ear like our cows and a white suit like a creamery worker. We went after him to hear what the Boss said, and Jim was singing into a yoke as loud as he was able – the house was shaking with it. Martin took the yoke off him, wiped it with his sleeve, shut his eyes and opened his mouth. ' "The Fields of Athenry",' says Jess, wagging her tail. 'Me favourite.'

Just as the Boss noticed Martin, he began to sing:

'Hug me! H-h-h-hug me till you crack my heart!
Kiss me! K-k-k-kiss me till I fall apart!'

It was much worse than the foxhounds. Me and Jess went back to the henhouse in a hurry and tried to sleep. I heard next day that the Boss tried to stop the noise machine and fused all the lights. After that, they sat in the dark, doing away with the sandwiches and singing 'The Old Bog Road' and 'Galway Bay'. One of the sheepdog men had brought his old dog, Ted, with him. He's deaf, so he was able to stand it. He came out and told us what was happening. 'Your Boss proposed a toast to Yank,' says he.

'I like toast,' says I. 'The Missis gives me the burnt bits. Is there any left?'

'Grow up, Shep,' says Ted. 'This kind of toast is to do with drink. You take a sup and say "*Slainte!*" or "The bitches, God bless 'em!" or "Here's to Yank!" Anything you like. Then you drink some more.'

'It sounds kind of childish to me,' says I.

'It is,' says Ted. 'Your Missis is crying over Yank going away, nobody can move for tangled wires and there isn't a candle in the house. I'll stay out here, it's safer.'

He soon went to sleep, but I stayed awake a long time, wondering. I like my people to behave in ways I can understand.

TWENTY-FIVE

THE party went on all night. They had stout with their cornflakes for breakfast. I brought in the cows and the Missis milked them; she was not in a good humour. Martin went home early because Julia and Peejay was on their own. He was supposed to come back and milk, but he didn't. Maybe he forgot. He came over around dinner-time, and all his fine green hair was clipped off him. He has green stubble now with red roots. He doesn't take his cap off if he can help it.

When he got here, the Missis had a big pile of rubbish outside the door. There was bottles, mostly broken, a big tangle of wire that Irish Stew left after them, newspapers – all kinds of things. 'I'm delighted to see you, even if you did leave me the cows to milk,' says the Missis. 'Now you can take all this old rubbish and dump it.'

'Where?' says Martin.

'I don't know where, and I don't care,' says the Missis, not like herself at all. She went in and banged the door after her.

Yank and the Boss was still in bed; they could be heard snoring.

Martin loaded all the rubbish into the tractor box,

and I lepped up in the cab with him. Things was all wrong at home. 'Good lad, Shep,' says Martin. 'We'll leave them to their hangovers.' I asked Jess since what was hangovers, and she says they're the men on the dole who lean on Coolcoffin Bridge all day, watching the river. Could she be wrong, I wonder?

We weren't long driving down to the place by the river which is where broken bottles and tins and dead bicycles end up. It was all levelled out and there was a notice: PICNIC AREA: NO DUMPING. Poor Martin, he didn't know what to do, so he drove into Coolcoffin. Now *Bord Failte*, or the Faulty Board as they call it around here, are going mad over being tidy. They cleaned up the fine dump by the river. There's another notice outside the town which says, CEAD MILE FAILTE. Jess says this means, 'Keep Coolcoffin tidy.' I haven't the Irish meself – I was reared in the east.

On all the telegram poles they have bins nailed. They say *BRUSCAR* on one side, and LITTER on the other. I'm glad to say I never saw a litter in one. Anyway, they're too high for a bitch to get into and the wrong shape for puppies. They're all right for rubbish.

Martin drove right through Coolcoffin and filled them all up to the top. Then we went home, to Martin's house.

I had me dinner with Floosie, and I told her about the bins for puppies, but she said plastic bags was better. 'Oh, Floosie,' says I, 'plastic bags is terrible dangerous – anyone could get smothered in them. Jess won't have one on the place.'

'Shep, me old friend,' says Floosie, 'did you never hear about the anti-litter campaign? Go home and ask Jess about it.' I thought we'd better talk about something else.

'How are they going on with that baby?' says I. 'Is he walking around yet?'

' 'Deed he's not then,' says Floosie, 'he's twelve weeks old and not a stir out of him. He's well able to howl, though.'

'Twelve weeks?' says I, 'he'll be coming up for distemper injections soon. It looks as if they're going to keep him.'

'They always keep them,' says Floosie. 'Look at the camp down the road – crawling with them – you didn't think they were for sale, did you, Softy?'

'I didn't know,' says I. 'I don't know what they'd want with so many and another poor woman mightn't have even one to her name. Don't laugh at me, Floosie, and don't call me Softy – I don't like it.' But Floosie walked off, still laughing.

The next time I passed the camp down the road, I remembered what Floosie said. There's silver caravans longer than our house, with plastic flowers in the windows and more babies than you could count. There's more smells than you could count too, and there's an Alstation like Otto chained up there who can swear in ten languages, he told me. There's dogs loose as well, but anyone can tell they're underdogs.

Could you blame me for thinking the babies was for sale? Everything else is. There's radios and holy pictures and delf – all sorts of lovely things. The Missis won't buy anything from the traders, and I'll tell you why.

One day, we went to Galway with Martin in the car, and he kept us waiting a long time. Sheep are more in my line than shops and the Missis said her corns were at her, so we stayed in the car and went to sleep. It was a warm day and the window was open. All of a sudden, a man put his head in through the window and says he, very loud, 'Buy a blanket, lady?'

The Missis woke in a hurry, and she let out a screech. Now I'm not a savage dog, but if anyone upsets the Missis, the blood of me ancestors boils in me veins. These were very brave and noble animals called jackals. Me Mammy told me about them when I was a little pup. I gave one jump, up off the floor, and went for the man. At the same time, the Missis shut the window and trapped his head. He was lucky because his cap fell off and all I got was a mouthful of greasy cloth. I sat on the Missis's lap waiting for her to open the window again so I could get him, but she didn't. Women!

The Missis's ancestors were not jackals, but something a lot less brave. She put the two arms around me, and the tears was dripping down on me head. 'Oh Shep, Shep, you saved me life,' says she.

I was embarrassed. I said nothing.

TWENTY-SIX

BAD news – the worst yet! Yank enjoyed himself to pieces at the party, his ticket is cancelled and he's going to live here with us. Him and the Boss went on a pilgrimage to Lough Derg, but the Missis was in bad humour and said it was a pity they wouldn't go on a pilgrimage to the bog and bring her a few loads of turf. They arrived back in a bus with a whole clatter of nuns. After that, they went to Sligo for a symposium, which Jess tells me is some kind of pudding. I wouldn't blame the Missis for being mad with them – she makes the finest of puddings.

Yank

Mr O'Brien has given up trying to make a trial dog of Tiny, and sold him to Colonel Crankshaft who lives near us, at Castlecoffin, up on Coffin Hill. There's no castle on it any more, it's all collapsticated. There's just a little new house, smaller than ours.

Colonel Crankshaft doesn't do any work, except for cutting grass. He's at it every week – never gives a decent crop of hay time to grow. He has a workman called Dan, and some cattle, but no dog until now. Tiny soon got bored, slipped his collar and came home to us. He was there when the Boss got back from Sligo.

Next day, the Colonel came looking for him and the Boss handed him over. 'Maybe you didn't know his commands,' says the Boss.

'Lost on me, I'm afraid, ha, ha, I leave all that to Dan,' says the Colonel. 'Never commanded a dog in me life. Commanding a battery's more in my line, ha, ha.' He laughed some more and took Tiny away. Now how could any Christian command a battery? I know about batteries – you switch them on and off. The Boss had a battery fencer and Martin switched it on just as he was getting over it and the thorny wire stuck in his trousers. The battery was ticking away, and with every tick the Boss gave a bigger lep and a louder roar. Martin said it was for a joke he did it, but the Boss wasn't amused and sent him to the bog for the rest of the day.

I was surprised after that when the Missis bought some battery hens. They lived in cages and laid a fine lot of eggs for a while. Then, all of a sudden, they stopped. I suppose the batteries ran down and they weren't able to get any more, as the battery hens were sold after that and went away in a lorry. The next time, the Missis bought deep-litter hens. Deep-litter indeed! Chickens come in clutches, not litters. Even a hen should know that.

I wasn't surprised when Tiny joined me when I was bringing in the cows the same evening. He is a champion collar slipper.

'The old fool,' says Tiny, 'I could have gone clean through that collar, legs and all. He loosened it two holes.' He nipped a cow just to see her jump, and then the Boss spotted him.

He has a hole dug half way to hell under the henhouse. He's in it yet.

I was never as idle as this spring. The Boss sold his sheep when I was stolen because he had no dog to work them. Jess wouldn't, and he had no heart to buy another. He had a row with the Missis over going to Sligo, so Yank went to stay with Martin and Julia, and the Boss took me to Maam Cross to buy sheep.

When we came back, the Missis met us, all smiles. 'I'm after selling the eight pups, all to the one woman,' says she. 'I got cash, in case you're wondering, and I gave her the registration folder. She'll send it back when she thinks of names for them; she says you should have a prefix.'

'A pity she wouldn't mind her own business,' says the Boss, getting madder by the minute, 'I don't need injections, tell her.'

'It isn't injections,' says the Missis, 'It's your special kennel name, like Wiston Cap and Bosworth Coon. And you can't have "Coolcoffin", Jim Dolan has it taken.'

The Boss was so pleased when he saw the pile of money the pups made that he let the Missis write off to get a prefix. She chose 'Wisheen', the name of our farm. Me and the Boss thought no more about it. We was off every day practising for the trials with the new sheep. We was happy as Larry. One morning a letter came from Mrs O'More in Dublin, with the names she'd chosen. The Missis read it out:

1. Wisheen Woebegone
2. Wisheen Wanderlust
3. Wisheen Wayfarer
4. Wisheen Wishingwell
5. Wisheen Welltodo
6. Wisheen Wideawake
7. Wisheen Wendyhouse
and 8. Wisheen Wizardry.

'Those aren't names for dogs,' says the Boss. 'Why didn't she call them Shep and Dolly and Jess – decent names? Tell her to change them.'

The Missis said she couldn't, and they had a great argument, but in a day or two another letter came, from England this time. It seems that the Sheep Dog Society doesn't allow long names, and they sent back papers for:

1. Wisheen Woe
2. Wisheen Wan
3. Wisheen Way
4. Wisheen Wish
5. Wisheen Well
6. Wisheen Wid
7. Wisheen Wen
and 8. Wisheen Wiz.

'Serve her right,' says the Boss.
Jess was pleased because the puppies had gone.

Although when she's vexed, she has a habit of reminding me, 'I'm the mother of your pups, you know,' she soon tires of them. Even so, I thought it best not to mention the anti-litter campaign to her.

TWENTY-SEVEN

THE Boss was so pleased with the sheep he got in Connemara that he went back and bought twenty more. We took Jim Dolan's Irish Stew van, but they wouldn't all fit in, so we had to go again with Jamesy Quinn's trailer. Floosie came with us because Julia, Martin and Yank was gone to a heritage seminar. I asked Jess what that was, but even she didn't know. I expect Floosie does, but I find it wiser not to ask her questions.

They tell me Connemara is a beautiful place, but Floosie and me aren't that interested in scenery. We settled down in the back of the car for a chat. 'How's the mother of your puppies?' says Floosie.

'Which one?' says I.

'Jess, of course,' says Floosie, 'she's the only one who goes on and on about it.'

'She's well,' says I. I was thinking, although I'd never have mentioned it to Floosie, of a funny thing I heard the Boss tell Colonel Crankshaft when he came to collect Tiny again. He said I was a good stud dog. That's silly, because, given half a chance, who isn't? All the dogs in Coolcoffin are the finest of stud dogs . . .

'Wake up, Lover Boy, I was talking to you,' says

111

Floosie, giving me an unloving kind of nip. 'I'm telling you, Chris is out of prison. I wonder will he come for me.'

'Jess says you should forget him if you can,' says I. 'She says you shouldn't miss the chance to start afresh.'

The trouble with Floosie is, when she strips her teeth you don't know is she laughing or is she going to bite you. This time she bit me first (hard) and then she laughed and laughed, rolling on her back. 'Oh, poor old Jess,' says she. 'Go home and tell her I've been Born Again.' I was puzzled. I said nothing.

After a while, Floosie stopped laughing and went to sleep. I licked her face and she opened one eye. There was no sign of teeth, so I cleaned up her ears a little. She said nothing – I think maybe she liked it. It's hard to tell.

The Boss had left ten sheep after him on a hillside near a place called Recess. There was big bushes on the hill with pink flowers on them – they should be cleared away. A dog has no chance of a decent gather. We looked all over, but the sheep was gone. Then we went to see the man who sold them, and he said he hadn't been on the hill since – why should he? He said there was stray dogs going the road, he'd heard them barking last night.

'Didn't you think of my sheep?' says the Boss.

'You should have taken them all Saturday,' says the man. 'They're probably in the factory by now.'

'What do you think, Floosie?' says I.

'I thought I smelled Chris on the hill,' says she. 'He has an unusual scent.' She was right there. When the guards took him away, they opened all the windows in the squad car. We got help and went back to the hill and searched it all. I went one way, Floosie went the other. I found one sheep on his back with the feet up; he was alive still. The men had to carry him half a mile to the trailer, and as they lifted him in, he died, God rest him.

I knew he'd been worried, and there was the scent of a dog around. I felt I knew that dog. As for Chris, there were places where I held me breath. When we were ready to go, the Boss whistled for Floosie. But Floosie was gone.

Yank is back with us, and there's no peace at home any more. He seemed happy enough at Martin's, but it seems Martin and Julia aren't hitting it off too well. Floosie told me a while ago that Julia does a share of crying and Martin goes out and leaves her to it. Yank advised them to go to a Young Marrieds Advice Bureau and they went off to Galway for the day, leaving Peejay asleep and Yank minding him.

I was in the cowshed with the Boss when I saw Yank rushing by, holding Peejay about three feet in front of him, and Peejay howling his best. Yank was taking him down to the Missis. That night Martin and Julia must have met up with friends because they didn't come home at all. Peejay and Yank stayed with us. Julia came in the morning, and Yank ate holy hell out of her and told her Peejay was the boss of the pair of them. He's not going back any more.

Yank had never seen a sheepdog trial, and there was one on Sunday.

The Boss said he'd run me and Yank could drive. Him and Martin are supposed to share the car, but nobody asked Martin and Julia and Peejay did they want to come. This is the bad part. Yank watched the trial all day, and I knew before we set off for home he'd caught the Trial Bug. Now when the Boss caught it, it came on him gradual. We didn't notice much difference until he took a turn for the worse and gave it to the Missis. Yank is different. Jess says it's because of living in America – he has no resistance. He wouldn't come home until the last novice had given up trying to pen the last sheep in the dark.

The Boss went to sleep and snored. Earlier me and him was beaten by half a point. The Boss had a few things to say about the judge, but no judge is ever right for him. Yank wanted to get an instruction book for trialling, and he was asking about buying a good young dog. Everyone at the trial was trying to sell to him. 'What are you raving about?' says the Boss. 'You can't even bring in the cows with a dog.'

'Robert Sangster doesn't ride his Derby winners,' says Yank. 'You're a crowd of amateurs, Jack. I'll buy the right dog and get him trained by a professional, and we'll beat you all.'

'If we could find Floosie you need look no farther,' says the Boss. 'She's an International dog in the making.'

'Bah!' says Yank. 'You don't want a home-bred dog for this game. I'll enquire around for an imported one. Martin isn't getting all that cash off me now, the way he's carrying on. I'll keep a thousand back and buy a Scottish dog.'

There were two ads in the paper that week. One said, 'Lost, white bitch. Reward. Apply Kelly, Coolcoffin.' The other said, 'Urgently wanted, Scottish or

Welsh bred Border Collie for training to International standard. Price no object for the right animal. Apply Kelly, Coolcoffin.'

I wonder will they get many answers.

TWENTY-EIGHT

W E don't have a telephone here because the Boss says he doesn't want people ringing him up and catching him unawares before he has time to disentangle his thoughts. So all the answers to the two adverts came through the post. I thought it must be Christmas until I remembered we'd had it a few months back.

The Boss was vexed because ever since Thursday, people have been calling with lost white bitches; Sunday was the worst. You see, he forgot to say 'sheepdog' so it was mostly terriers that came. There was a greyhound I liked the look of as well. People aren't all straight and decent. Half those poor bitches told me they belonged to the ones that brought them. They were looking for the reward.

The letters covered the kitchen table on Friday. The Missis and Yank started to open them. The Boss looked at a couple, then he went out. Monday and Tuesday was the same. Wednesday, things were easing off; only fifteen letters, Yank said.

It seems April was a terrible month for losing white bitches, but none of them was Floosie. As for Yank's advert, you'd think every Border Collie in the country came out of Scotland or Wales. Some of them had their papers lost, or a little mistake had been made along the line so papers couldn't be got for them. Even so, every one was the best young dog in the country.

They started by burning all the letters from more than a hundred miles away, all the ones from women (the Boss's idea), all the ones looking for more than a thousand pounds and the ones we knew about already. I mean dogs we knew were vicious or blind or something. There was an awful lot left. 'I'll see this one first,' says Yank. 'The owner sounds like an honest man.' He read out:

Dear Mr Kelly,

My dog is a pedigree Border Collie from Wales. Duplicate papers might easily be obtained. The originals were lost in a shipwreck. This dog has power in abundance. He needs only the tuition of a handler like you, Mr Kelly, to bring out the true potential of this fine dog. I am offering him at the specially reduced price of £725. He may be seen here doing anything.

> Your obedient servant,
> James Joyce

'He doesn't sound like an honest man to me,' says the Boss, kindling his pipe, 'he sounds like a right hangman.'

'If he was a crook,' says Yank, 'he wouldn't have put in that bit about a shipwreck. He'd think I wouldn't believe it.'

'I don't believe it,' says the Boss.

After dinner, Yank went off to Connemara to see the dog. Julia came looking for the car to go to a Camogie Reunion, and the Boss said he was almost sorry for Yank. Chains wouldn't hold Julia when she's properly mad.

✪

I'd been thinking on and off of a message I found on a tree near Recess. I wasn't able to make it out at the time, but when I heard about the Welsh sheepdog, I understood it. BARK WAS HERE. Or rather, Bach, which is how they spell it in Wales for want of knowing better. That's why I wasn't really surprised when Yank came home after midnight, legless, and with Bark in the car.

You'd be talking about Tiny doing damage. He just slips collars and nips when he shouldn't. Bark tears down doors, digs up four stone weights and can break a strong chain if he gets a run at it. When Yank landed home, everyone was in bed. Me and Jess was in the stable, watching through the cracks in the door. The car went over the edge of the cement with two wheels of it and stopped. Yank climbed out on the high up side of it, letting the door bang after him. He had a bottle in his hand.

He went to the back door and spent a long time opening it, then he went up to bed.

'How could a decent man find it in himself to come home in that state?' says Jess.

'Never mind Yank,' says I. 'That's Bark in the car.' When Bark spotted us peeping through the door, he barked, but nobody came. I am descended from some noble jackals, but Bark told me once that his ancestors were red dragons – I can believe it. When he found he couldn't get out, he set about the inside of the car with his teeth. I wasn't able to watch – I went into the corner, but Jess barked and howled for the Boss. She has a soprano singing voice and she's learned to keep quiet at night. I suppose that's why the Boss heard her.

The door burst open and the Boss rushed out, shouting. Then he stopped in the middle of a shout; he'd seen the car and Bark going mad inside. He said a few bad words and opened the car door – I think he meant to catch Bark. I suppose if you're half asleep, it's hard to catch a black dog on a dark night – especially if he tries to bite you. I don't blame the Boss at all for letting him go. Then he got a flashlamp and looked at the way the car was left, with one wheel right off the ground.

'How can a good clean-living man lower himself to use such language?' says Jess. 'Don't listen, Shep.' Don't listen! He could have been heard in Clifden. Still, he didn't wake Yank, although the Missis came down in her nightdress with her hair wrapped round bits of plastic. The Missis began to cry, and the two of them went into the house. Me and Jess cried out of sympathy until the Boss leaned his top half out of the window and asked us not to.

'I'm thankful there are no puppies within earshot,' says Jess.

❖

The next day, the Boss took the car to Galway for new seats. Yank is paying for them. Yank moved his things back into Martin's house. Then he went to look for Bark in a hired car. I thought he'd have to go back to Connemara; I heard Chris's curlew whistle as plain as anything just after Bark got away. Yank never saw Chris before. He'd have known Floosie, of course, but she wasn't around.

That week, the ad in the paper said, 'Lost, white sheepdog bitch and valuable black male Border Collie, answers name "Bach." Guards notified, substantial reward.'

Yank gave £700 in cash for Bark. Chris makes the best of poteen, and poor Yank took so much he thought there were two dogs running and asked Chris would he sell both. Then he had to pretend he was joking. The guards went to see Chris and didn't find any dogs or any poteen either. Chris said he was sorry about Bark, but if people got drunk and let valuable dogs loose at night in strange places they must expect to lose them. He's a right hangman, like the Boss said.

The sheep are lambing, and Martin isn't here to mind them. He's gone to a Sheep Handling Week at Castlebar. Julia is hopping mad because Peejay has the measles and Yank is afraid to help her mind him, for fear he'd catch them.

Last night, we had to get the vet to one of the ewes. The Boss went to Coolcoffin on his bike for the vet, and the ewe lambed all by herself when he'd gone. I thought she winked at me. The Missis was there and she was highly delighted, but the Boss wasn't as pleased as all that. It was two in the morning, so the vet wasn't sorry he had nothing to do. The Missis invited him in for some hot punch. So in we went, and the Missis mixed whiskey and lemonade in a saucepan, with marmalade to sweeten it because she was out of honey, which the Boss likes best.

The Boss was sitting in his old saggy chair with his head in his hands. 'Ah, drink it yourself, Mam, I don't want it,' says he. I was sure he must be dying when I heard that. I looked up at him and he was all red spots around the jaws and more coming by the minute. So now the Boss is in bed with the measles, Julia is minding him as well as Peejay when she remembers, and me and the Missis is looking after the sheep. I never thought I'd be glad to see Martin home, but it'll be great to get help. Even Yank would be better than nothing.

TWENTY-NINE

I was desperate sick since; I thought I was going to die. The trouble was that nobody had much time for me lately.

Martin came back from the Sheep Handling Week when all the ewes were done lambing, the cows were calving and the Boss still in bed. As for Yank, he was away all day and every day. He said he'd find Bark if it was the last thing he did, and the Missis said she didn't care if it was. She was very snappish altogether. Jess said they should agree among themselves and help one another. 'It's all very well for you,' says I, 'sitting on a big pile of oaten straw, getting two meals a day and never lifting a paw to help anyone.'

'Aren't you very cranky?' says she. 'I suppose it's because you're not as young as you were. Your nose is all grey now.'

I do try to see things her way, and I never think of Floosie when Jess is there, because she *knows*. 'I wonder what happened to the old white slave?' says Jess. 'Got herself shot by this, I dare say. There's a gang of dogs worrying sheep over in Glengombeen.'

'Floosie's anti blood sports now,' says I. 'I doubt if Bark is, though.'

122

'Poor Bark,' says Jess. 'He came from a broken home.' I suppose she means something like the silver caravan the tree fell on last year. I was feeling too sick to bother to ask.

There's trouble over the Wisheen pups too. Mrs O'More has found out the Kennel Club won't register them. She meant to sell them for big money for shows and now she can't. They're getting big and she lives in a two-roomed flat with the eight of them, so I suppose it might be crowded. Anyway, she says the Missis misled her and she's going to take steps – whatever that means. I hope she doesn't take them in this direction.

If she got the Missis to pay it wouldn't be fair. Mikey Goggin up the road buys whole litters at £10 each and sells them for £50 a pup. He makes out they are all out of his good bitch, Bess. She was supposed to have had forty-seven puppies last year and thirty-nine the year before. Most of Mikey's dogs are really Borderline Collies.

I felt worse and worse. If only the Boss was better, I thought, everything would be all right. I wondered was I getting the measles – you wouldn't see spots through hair. Jess said dogs didn't get measles. 'It might be the Parvo,' says she.

'I could die of that,' says I, 'and then how would the Boss manage? And you might take it as well.'

'I wouldn't,' says Jess. 'I got a booster last time I was expecting. If it isn't Parvo, it's likely some germ you caught off that Floosie.'

I was vexed. I said nothing.

It was three days before the Missis noticed I was off me feed. Jess had been eating me dinner for me. 'Waste not, want not,' says she. The Missis was in a right state when she saw how sick I was. She ran into the house for the Boss, and he came out with his topcoat over his nightshirt, his tackety boots and his bare legs. They were still all spots.

'Will you stop crying and get the vet,' says he. 'We want a cure, not an obituary in *Working Sheepdog News.*'

'What's an obituary, Jess?' says I, very faint and weak.

'It's getting fixed so you can't have any more puppies,' says she. I thought I'd have to get better quick.

The vet was a long time coming, and I was lying inside the stable door, wanting to be out. When you're as sick as that, you want to be alone, and I'd have been happier under the henhouse. 'I don't know where they'll get another dog like you,' says Jess.

'I hope they won't have to,' says I.

'Never mind, Shep,' says Jess. 'Remember you always did your best. You'll leave Coolcoffin a little better than you found it. That's as much as can be expected of any dog.'

I thought about Floosie, the first time I met her, looking for fleas. 'Shut your gob,' says I. 'You give me a pain.'

'Shep! I never thought I'd hear you talk in that low, common way. Those might be your last words,' says Jess.

'I'll say one more thing,' says I. 'If you're right about me, I hope you'll make some kind of an effort to help out with the work. They haven't the money to buy another dog like me and you know it. That's me biggest worry. Goodbye.'

I said no more and Jess went into the corner, whimpering like a puppy.

When the vet came, the first thing he said was, 'Take that old bitch away and tie her up somewhere.' The Boss had got dressed and he led her away. 'Goodbye, me poor old Shep,' says she. 'Cheer up – there's nothing so bad it couldn't be worse.'

'Come on out of that,' says the Boss.

The Missis made a bed of straw for me, with the pig-lamp to keep me warm. The vet gave me three injections, and left a bottle of pills for me. 'He should live,' says he, 'but I wish I'd been called in sooner. He must have been off his feed for days.' The Missis was crying; she said nothing.

The Missis

I lay under the lamp for two days, and the vet came twice more. I began to get better, and Jess came to talk to me through the cracks in the door. 'I hope you're properly thankful for your miraculous recovery,' says she.

'I haven't recovered yet,' says I.

'The Boss will be hard set to pay the vet,' says Jess. 'He was put to the pin of his collar taking you to Wales last year and England the year before. Only for the fine money my puppies made, it couldn't be done at all.'

'You're no comfort to me, Jess,' says I. 'I wish you'd go away. Help the Missis with the hens – you're good at that.'

'Ah, now,' says Jess, 'we all know it would be a different story if that Floosie was spending all her spare time trying to cheer you up.' She went away, and I didn't see her again all day, saints be praised.

I know now what made me ill. I had an argument with a Rottweiler and he bit me neck. Jess told me Rottweiler was German for 'vile rotter,' so that's what I called him, having no German. In fact, I still don't know what *achtung* means. The sore turned septic and it was hidden by long hair. I couldn't get at it to lick it, and Jess didn't fancy the job. It was blood-poisoning I had, not the Parvo or the Measles.

I'm glad. I wouldn't like Floosie, if I ever see her again, to hear I'd had the measles.

THIRTY

WHEN the Boss got well, he had to work hard to make up for the time he lost when he was sick. One day, he went to the town and bought a gun for the sheep. 'Surely to God,' says the Missis, 'bad and all as the poor things are, you're not going to shoot them?'

'Have sense, will you? It's a yoke for dosing them,' says the Boss. 'You can dose six hundred in an hour,' says he.

The Missis had a think, then she got a pencil and thought some more. 'You must be wrong,' says she. 'That means you could do ours in two minutes.'

'Maybe I could at that,' says the Boss, 'if I had a bit of help catching them. Only for Shep, I'd have to retire.' I was hardly better of the blood-poisoning, and things were still all wrong. I wasn't happy because the Boss was in a bad temper. The Boss was in a bad temper because the Missis was worried. The Missis was worried because Julia was up here night, noon and morning, cribbing about Martin who kept going to Galway without taking her and Peejay.

Now my Boss is as brave as a lion; he fears neither man nor beast but he dreads Julia. When Martin takes the car she comes down here. She used to carry Peejay and the Boss couldn't hear her coming, but now Peejay is big and more like the Boss than ever, God bless him, she wheels him in the pram. When we hear the pram, me and the Boss go quietly out of the front door which wasn't used these years. We go to the pub.

The day we got the gun, we were rightly caught. We'd been working an hour and got about half the sheep done when in walks Julia with Peejay in her arms. 'Take the child in to Mam, get an old pair of pull-ups and give me a hand,' says the Boss.

'Don't you care,' says Julia, 'that your only son is going to be up on a platform with Euphoria Ryan and the Sobsisters?'

'What are you on about? It's mad you are if you ask me,' says the Boss.

'He's the one that's mad,' says Julia, 'off singing twice a week with Irish Stew, that was bad enough, but now he's singing his new song with the Sobsisters in Galway. Him and Euphoria is singing it and we know all about *her*.' I sometimes think Julia is a little like Jess – not as pretty though.

'I never heard of any Euphoria Ryan,' says the Boss. 'Martin's a good singer, always was, like his Da.' He whistled a few bars of 'Spancilhill'.

'You want to see our home wrecked, our marriage broke up and me and Peejay out begging on the roads, I suppose,' says Julia. Her face was very red.

'Oh, get the hell out! Go in to Mam and leave me in peace,' roars the Boss. Julia got the hell out and the Boss threw his stick at me, which he didn't do since the year before last. He missed, and anyway I didn't hold it against him.

❂

Yank is home again after searching the country for Bark. He says Chris is gone and his house locked up. The Boss is building a new cement wall at the end of the silage yard. He has Patsy Foley helping him, and Martin is kept going fetching and carrying for them. He's sulky and says nothing. The job is taking a long time because they forgot to leave holes for the wind to blow through and it all fell down, so they had to start again. The Boss got a bill and he nearly lost his life. He's paying Patsy by the hour for work that was done twice, but there was no way out of it, he had to pay up.

'How can a man live?' says he. 'The sheep is gone to hell, the milk is levied and petrol is gone up again.'

'I could keep you all in luxury, only for the one I'm married to,' says Martin, speaking low, with his eyes on the cement block he was carrying.

'Why did you marry her so? You had the cream of Coolcoffin to choose from,' says the Boss. 'You have her now, so get on with that wall and less old chat.'

Martin dropped the block. It broke. 'I hadn't a right grip of it,' says he.

'And you talk about keeping us!' says the Boss in a right rage. 'You couldn't keep ferrets!' He called me and we went for a walk. The Boss can't lift blocks because he has a hernia and his insides might drop out if he did. When we got back, there was no sign of Martin. Patsy was having to hand the blocks to himself.

'Where's Martin?' says the Boss.

'Gone for a bath,' says Patsy, 'and to dress for the evening.'

'A bath at half three in the afternoon?' says the Boss. 'It's in the Mental Home he should be.'

'Didn't he tell you?' says Patsy, 'he's off to Ennis.'

'Ennis?' the Boss was only able to gasp.

'There's a big competition on, to find Voice Ireland '93,' says Patsy.

'The world is gone mad,' says the Boss. Martin didn't even tell the Missis in case she'd tell the Boss, but he has Julia partly tamed, and she went with him in a new green dress.

Yank and Peejay was here, in bad tempers the two of them, at teatime. Yank has to stay in case he gets word of Bark. He has nothing to do. He could help build the wall, as he has no hernia that I know of, but he says he left that kind of work behind him when he left Ireland. The Boss says, 'You came back to it – nobody made you.'

'It's me back,' says Yank, 'I slips discs awful easy. If that happened, you'd have me here solid months, above on the bed in agony.' No more was said about the wall.

Peejay is getting teeth. You'd think it was a new thing, getting teeth. 'Look at them,' says the Missis, 'clusters of them, sharp as razors.'

'Famous,' says the Boss, not looking. 'It's the deception I don't like. Why didn't Martin tell us he won heats in the singing at Glenamaddy and Moycullen? He gave us no chance to hear him.'

'Be fair, Jack,' says Yank, 'Julia says she told you and you didn't bother your head listening to her, but shouted out and frightened the souls out of her and Peejay. Why don't we all have a jar to brighten us up?'

'You haven't well finished your tea,' says the Boss, 'you'll be an alcoholic before long, the way you're carrying on.'

Yank opened his mouth to answer, he was mad because the Boss drinks twice as much as he does, but the Missis, who hates a row, butted in. 'I wonder what's on the telly,' says she.

Yank opened the *RTE Guide*. 'We might have missed it,' says he. 'The semi-final of Voice Ireland coming live from Ennis. This is going to be good.'

THIRTY-ONE

IT's a funny thing how people alter, all in a minute. Dogs don't change much – well Floosie might, but she's different.

We had an hour to wait before the singing programme started, and except for Peejay, nobody once stopped talking about Martin, how he was an ornament to the parish, the pet of his family, his Dada's pride, his Mammy's joy . . . I lay under the table and wondered were we thinking about the same lad. 'Me favourite nephew,' says Yank.

'He could sing like a blackbird at three years of age,' says the Boss.

'I always said he'd make his mark in the world,' says the Missis. 'Peejay'll make a singer too, he has a great pair of lungs.'

' 'Tis all inherited from me,' says the Boss.

'Ten minutes more,' says Yank. He turned on the news, then he jumped up out of his chair. 'Will you look at us all,' says he, 'going to watch Martin winning in black and white. We'd miss half the good of it. We'll go down to Jamesy Quinn's quick.'

Jamesy has a colour television. We didn't delay a minute. Martin had the car, so the Boss rode his bike, Yank ran, and the Missis trotted behind carrying

Peejay. I followed, not wanting to miss it, but when we got to the house, they all went in and shut the door after them.

Jamesy's dog Carlo ran up and down on his chain, which is how he passes his time, and laughed at me. 'You're soon forgotten when one of their own is on the telly,' says he. I sat on the step and wished I'd stayed at home. If I'd kept quiet under the table they wouldn't have noticed me, and in their rush they forgot to turn the telly off and lock the door when they left.

I sat a long time listening to them inside. I heard a noise machine like Irish Stew only much worse, then I heard a voice a little like Floosie's when there's a full moon and the Boss isn't around: 'Hug me, h-h-h-hug me till you crack my heart . . .' Then Martin, singing like a madman.

'Carlo,' says I, 'do you know "Howling the Blues"? What the Firedogs used to sing?'

'I do of course,' says Carlo.

'Come on then,' says I, 'They'll think we're part of the orchestra.' So we sang at the tops of our voices and nobody noticed. The old songs is the best.

I'd been asleep a long time when they all came out of Jamesy's house, delighted with themselves. Martin had won the semi-final, and they'd had a drink or two to celebrate. It was around three in the morning. The Boss had the song learned off. 'It isn't so bad when you get used to it,' says he. Him and Yank sang all the way home. Jamesy Quinn forgot he was at home already and came too. The Boss forgot his bike and left it after him.

133

There hasn't been a gate into our yard since Martin had a misunderstanding with the tractor last year. The piers are still there, solid cement, three feet square, waiting for a new gate. Around one of the piers was a chain like you might use to pull a tractor out of a bog. On the other end of the chain was Bark. He was wearing a collar made of five or six flat steel chains and it was fastened with a padlock.

Bark isn't easy to see at night, and I suppose whoever left him there thought we might fall over the chain or drive over Bark. They'd put a cross of red, luminous paper on his forehead, and that was what we saw when the Boss shined his flash-lamp. The Missis screamed out in a fright. The Boss stopped singing and stared. Yank took the lamp from him and shined it on Bark and the chain and the pier of the gate. 'I never thought he'd come home on his own,' says he.

'Tied himself up, too,' says the Boss in a nasty voice.

'I wonder how will we free him,' says Yank. 'We could lift the chain over the pier, but there's a lock on that as well.' (There was – a padlock as big as a saucer.) 'Have you a hacksaw, Jack?'

'Leave him where he is and have sense,' says the Boss. 'Do you want to lose him again? We'll think what to do in the morning. Come on, lads, "H-h-h-hug me baby, hug me tight . . ." ' They went into the house, singing away as happy as larks.

'You're a right one,' says I to Bark. 'You made the Missis cry over the damage you did to our car. I wonder you had the nerve to come home.'

'Not my idea,' says Bark, 'there's no excitement round here – no wonder you're a dull dog. No, don't start growling, listen. Chris took me that night, and the guards are mad looking for him. Yank's been telling them he has a cousin a detective in the States and he never fails to catch a thief. Poor Chris had to leave the grand house he found empty, and he has such a hatred taken to Yank, he thought he'd give me back to him.'

Just then, we heard a lot of shouting going on up at the house. Bark barked and I went to see what happened. I said they left the telly on and the door unlocked, well, someone had taken telly and all away with them. They'd taken all the silver cups me and the Boss won, but not the statue we won on *One Dog and His Man*. They'd pulled out the dresser drawers and got nothing. They missed £30 in the teapot we don't use. They'd taken the Boss's new book, *How to Perfect Your Outfield Work*, and half a hogget ewe out of the freezer. They'd taken Yank's raincoat, his sunglasses, his camera and his big white hat. They'd taken half a bag of 'Collywobbles' and the gun for dosing the sheep.

They left the key of Bark's chain on the kitchen table.

THIRTY-TWO

CHRIS got away dressed up like Yank. The two of them are small little men, but Yank smells a lot better. The farm has been creeping with guards for days and I'm lying low.

'What were you doing loose?' says I to Jess. 'I thought you were locked up that night.'

'I was minding the house, seeing as nobody else was,' says she.

'You made a bad job of it,' says I.

'Chris picked up a hayfork when he saw me,' says Jess, 'so I went round to the back of the barn and barked to frighten him. Being valuable, I was afraid he might steal me. He had that Floosie in the car – I could smell her.' I spent the rest of the day under the henhouse.

Yank didn't lose the rest of his dollars, because he carries them everywhere. He felt bad, because it was him buying Bark that started the trouble, so he went to Galway and bought us a colour telly and a book for the Boss called *Famous Trials*. The book is about criminals, not about real trials at all, so he's changing it. He still has the Trial Bug, real bad. He bought a doorbell that barks too, but the Boss won't have it. He says it'll only frighten the postman and he never

136

heard of a burglar ringing the doorbell.

As for Bark, he's still chained in the gateway. Yank bought him a kennel to sleep in but he has it ripped asunder. He has no gratitude and he says he never feels cold. Yank unlocks him every day and Bark takes him for a walk. Yank says it reminds him of water-skiing and the exercise keeps him fit, but anyone can see he doesn't really enjoy it. Bark loves it.

With all the excitement, Martin was forgotten at first. He didn't come to milk in the morning – the Boss thought he would, the harmless man. He has to sing once more, in Dublin, and it's the talk of the countryside. There was a picture of him in the paper with Euphoria, who is thin, fair and shaggy. They are holding the cup they won in Ennis. Behind them, Julia, in the new dress, is smiling and looking fit to kill the pair of them. Julia isn't able to sing.

If Martin and Euphoria win in Dublin, they might be in the *Eurovision*, which is a kind of *One Man and His Song*. 'How proud of Martin you must be,' says Yank to the Boss.

The Boss had hold of the paper and he was grinding his teeth.

'Listen to this,' says he. ' "Euphoria, a tall, willowy, blonde nineteen-year-old, says, 'All the credit rests with Martin. He sings like an angel, but he's just a simple country boy at heart.' Sobsisters Imelda, Concepta and Ann-Siobhàn clustered round the handsome, redheaded . . ." ' Then the Boss said several words the Missis doesn't let him use in the house, and opened the door of the range to put the paper inside.

Yank took it off him and smoothed it out. 'Take it

easy,' says he. 'It says here that him and the Euphoria one are just good friends.'

I was shivering under the table. I'd have been gone, only the door was shut. The Boss was near foaming at the mouth. Then the door opened, and in walked Julia, red in the face and setting down her feet as if she was planting cabbages. The Boss jumped up. 'That-was-a-fine-thing-Martin-did-you-must-be-proud-of-him,' says he, all in one breath. He went round Julia and out of the door, saying he had to sort cattle.

I slipped through the door after him, nearly getting caught in it because he was in such a rush to shut it for fear of Julia. We went to the pub. While we were out, Bark bit a guard.

We had a right time at the pub, because when you've been broken into, everybody stands you a half one. I worried about the Boss biking home, but we were lucky and got a lift home in the squad car. The sergeant told us a young guard was gone into Galway Outpatients with his leg after Bark biting him, but he wasn't too bothered about him. He's only new out of Templemore, the place where they breed them.

When we got home, the sergeant asked Yank to come outside for a chat. He told him Bark would have to be shot, as biting guards is a capital offence. Yank unlocked Bark and put his hand in his mouth to show how gentle he really is. Bark closed his teeth gently and squoze. Yank kept grinning away and the sergeant says to him, 'Where did you get that chain?'

'It was left with the dog,' says Yank, blinking his eyes and putting his hand in his pocket.

'It's new,' says the sergeant, 'and so are the pad-
locks. They'll be easy traced. A clue – it was a good
thing Guard Egan got the bite in a way, drew me
attention to that chain.'

'I hope he doesn't get tetanus,' says Yank.

'Ah, there's small fear of him,' says the sergeant,
all excitement. He thought he was going to catch
Chris as a trophy for Coolcoffin before the detective
from Galway arrived. 'Come on, Paddy, and bring
the dog. We'll call at all the shops where Chris might
have bought that chain. Have you a muzzle?' Yank
had. He couldn't have left Bark after him without the
chain, or he'd have been gone again. 'He's a funny
looking sheepdog, where'd he come from?' says the
sergeant, as Yank put it on.

Chris

'Wales,' says Yank, looking at his hand.

'Strap that muzzle good and tight,' says the sergeant.' They make out it's a beautiful country, Wales. I'm thinking of visiting it meself this year.'

'There'll be a welcome in the valleys if you do, boyo,' says Bark, as well as he could for leather. I *think* that's what he said.

Yank and the sergeant had no trouble finding the shop where Chris bought Bark's chain. The man remembered selling it because he asked Chris what it was for and Chris said it was to tie up a dog, so he thought he was joking. He said he was riding a bike, so they think they'll find him soon.

Bark isn't to be shot after all, on account of his chain being a clue.

THIRTY-THREE

IT wasn't until Yank and the sergeant was gone that the Missis thought to ask Julia what was wrong with her. I was under the table and the Boss had gone for a rest after the half ones. 'Martin lied to me,' says Julia.

'Don't tell me about it,' says the Missis, 'don't bring your troubles to me. You're a grown woman with a child of your own.' Julia had Peejay with her and the two of them began to cry. The Missis was lighting the range, which had gone out. 'Listen, Julia,' says she, 'I feel very proud of Martin and what he did in Ennis. It's yourself is behaving like a child, and you're teaching Peejay to cry. He never cries with me. Would you ever get the range going while I go for the cows with Shep? Dada's tired; he's on the bed.'

'I will,' says Julia, 'but first I'll tell you what your fine son said to me. He said he was going to Athlone for a slurry-handling demonstration.'

'I see no harm in that,' says the Missis. 'Not if it's the kind of thing you enjoy.'

'I saw Jim Dolan this morning,' says Julia, 'and he says Martin was taking lessons in break-dancing in Athenry that day.'

'The liar,' says the Missis. 'There's bad blood in the Dolans – his father was the same.' She sat back on her heels. 'What's break-dancing, anyway?' says she.

'They stand on their heads and spin,' says Julia.

'G'way,' says the Missis, 'there's something new every day. Martin would be better at the slurry handling.'

Julia let a bawl out of her and ran out into the yard. I saw that the fire had gone out again. Me and the Missis left it the way it was and went for the cows. We could hear Julia and Peejay crying all the way to the end of the lane.

❂

There's no word from the guards about Chris so far, and Yank and the Boss is going to the trials again. They didn't take Bark, but I won three cups for the Boss which will help to make up for the ones that was taken. Yank asked all the dog trainers he met would they train Bark. 'We will not,' says they.

On Sunday, me and the Boss went to Glengombeen, which is our nearest trial. Mr O'Brien won the novice class with Mist, who is a daughter of mine. He still wants to buy me although me best days is over. He's the best trainer I know. 'We have a dog at home you couldn't train,' says the Boss.

'Will he work? Is he well-bred?' says Mr O'Brien.

'He's the keenest worker I ever saw, and has breeding to beat the band,' says the Boss, 'and I'll bet you a pup by Shep to a pup out of Mist that you couldn't train him to take four quiet sheep around a novice course.'

'What age is he?' says Mr O'Brien.

'Only two,' says the Boss.

'Done,' says Mr O'Brien. He called at our place that evening on his way home, and there was Bark, standing up on the tractor trailer. Yank was holding his chain and staring straight at him.

'What are you at now?' says the Boss.

'It's this book I got,' says Yank, *The Power of the Human Eye: Taming and Training Wild Animals.* You stare at them until they look away. After that, you have the mastery over them.' Me and the Boss and Mr O'Brien all watched while Yank fixed his human eyes (small and greeny blue) on Bark's yellowy brown ones. At last, Yank looked away. 'I'll have another read and try again,' says he. 'I must be doing it wrong.'

'Denis here is going to train him for you,' says the Boss.

'I'm beginning to regret what I said,' says Mr O'Brien, 'but a bet's a bet. My God,' says he, 'what kind of a collar is that? The poor dog.' He turned the chain collar with the padlock round and round. 'I'll fix him up with something different,' says he, 'his neck is getting sore. It's only a month since you nearly lost Shep with a sore neck.' Bark growled, looking at him sideways.

'He doesn't exactly bite,' says Yank, 'but he might take your arm or your leg between his teeth, and if you were to move, he might sink them in a little. He's not bad tempered, only playful.'

'I see,' says Mr O'Brien. 'I don't think his temper is going to be my biggest problem.' He took hold of Bark by his chain. 'The poor dog,' says he again, and he loaded him into his little trailer.

Yank had to run down the lane after him with Bark's key.

THIRTY-FOUR

BARK had been with Mr O'Brien a fortnight and Floosie had been missing for three months when the squad car arrived in our yard. The sergeant was in it – him that was here before.

'Good day to you,' says Yank. 'Caught Chris, have you? No? He's too sharp for you country cops.'

The sergeant walked past without answering him. 'I think we have your dog,' says he to the Boss. 'We had a line on Chris – he's been living in an abandoned caravan. He legged it a couple of days ago and left the dog tied under the caravan. We found her when we heard the pups crying.'

'Pups?' says the Boss. 'Has she pups?'

'How could they cry if she hadn't?' says the sergeant.

'Did you bring them?' says the Boss. He'd been at his dinner, but he got up from the table and left it after him.

'You couldn't bring them,' says the sergeant, 'that one is like a devil. Come with us and bring them you. Bring your own car.' So Yank drove, and they let me come along to pacify Floosie if she was troublesome.

We were an hour driving to the caravan – it was

away off, down a narrow road; the traders left it behind. I was out of the car in a flash and went to look underneath. Floosie was chained to the axle. She was a right mess, you could count her ribs. She had seven puppies with her, about three weeks old. There was a dish of water where she could reach it, but no food.

'Hello, Dreamy Eyes,' says Floosie, grinning at me the same as ever. 'Has the Boss brought anything to eat with him? The maid forgot to bring me breakfast.'

Floosie never liked the Boss much, but she let him take the puppies and put them on a bed of straw in the car boot. Then she jumped in after them. The puppies were as black as soot except for one little white one like herself.

We hadn't any food for her, so we stopped at a little shop, but they'd no bread or dogfood. Floosie drank three litres of milk, and ate two Swiss rolls and six queen-cakes with pink icing. Then she went to sleep. We took her to Martin's house, on account of her and Jess not agreeing.

When she was settled down, and the puppies sucking away like little machines, I says to Floosie, 'Aren't they very black?'

'Lark isn't,' says Floosie, 'she's very white. No colour bar here,' says she.

Floosie has travelled a fair bit and she often has me puzzled. I know what a bar is of course, none better, and I suppose you could say she was serving drink. Even so, I'm not such a fool that I don't know she can only do milk. To change the subject I said, 'Have you names on them? Jess doesn't bother with names – she says it's the nature that counts.'

'She would,' says Floosie. 'These lads here are Gwilym, Dylan and Jenkyn, that's Ceri and Evan in the middle, and Boosie and little Lark at the back.' I thought they were funny names. I said nothing.

The Boss and Julia came out with soup they'd warmed for Floosie. 'We'll never find homes for all those little mongrels,' says Julia. 'I wonder what breed they are.'

The Boss picked up Jenkyn and looked at him. Jenkyn looked him straight in the eye. His eyes are still blue, but they have a wild look, and his ears are set low down on the sides of his head. He yowled and wriggled and bit the Boss's thumb. 'They're sheepdogs all right,' says the Boss, putting him down. ' 'Tis easy known. They have the best of breeding.'

I know now what break-dancing is. They go on until they break something. Martin has broken his neck. Now, I thought a broken neck meant the Missis crying and a funeral at the river – or in the garden if he was a good worker. Not now, they say. Martin is in hospital in Galway. He is going to get better, but he'll miss the final of the singing in Dublin. Euphoria Ryan and all the Sobsisters went to see him in hospital, and there was a bit about it in the evening paper. They say he'll be wearing a collar when he comes home. I know Julia doesn't trust him, but I didn't think she'd go so far as to tie him up. I'm sure it must be a lie.

I'll say this for Julia, she doesn't forget to mind Floosie. She's mad about her and says she'd travel to the jaws of death for her. Floosie is still wretched looking, with her hair coming out and scabs on her face, but she's in great spirits.

Dylan, Gwilym, Evan, Ceri, Jenkyn and Boosie are getting fatter and blacker and woollier every day. Little Lark is the cutest thing you ever saw, snow white with dark eyes and a black spot on the top of her head.

We're saving hay just now, so Yank has to work. They say he has his passage booked. There's no time to take me to trials, so I spend me spare time with Floosie. Jess is not pleased about this. 'You were the one who was always saying Floosie should have puppies like everybody else,' says I.

'I know her sort,' says Jess, 'she's rotten to the core.' I didn't like that, so I went down the lane to see Floosie.

'For a dog that doesn't like puppies,' says Floosie, 'you come down here a lot.'

'You don't like them either. What about the anti-litter campaign?' says I.

'They could be worse,' says Floosie. 'I never reared any before. Tell Jess I'm discovering the joys of motherhood.'

'I will,' says I, 'you're rearing them great. Look at the bloom on them.'

'The better I rear them, the sooner I'll be rid of the little devils,' says Floosie. 'I want to grow me coat and get me figure back before Chris comes for me.'

'You'd never go back to Chris after what he did,' says I. 'He left you and the whole family to starve.'

'He did not,' says Floosie, stripping her teeth. 'He went when he knew the guards would be sure to find me. Will you tell me, Softy, how would you escape from a carload of guards on a bike, with all you owned, a stolen dog and a litter of pups?'

You're making excuses for him,' says I. 'He's rotten to the core.'

'Now where did you pick up that expression? No don't tell me, I'm after guessing. Wouldn't you go along with your Boss if he did it to you?'

'He wouldn't,' says I, 'but if he did, I'd know something happened so he couldn't help it. I'd follow him into hell and out again.'

'We're a right pair of eejits, but sure, it's our nature,' says Floosie.

It was then I heard Jess crying and howling down at the farm. 'Yow-ow-ow-ow-ow ... Bark is dead, Bark is dead, Bark is dead! Wow-oo, wow-oo, wow-ooooo ... Poor Bark, poor Bark, poor Bark. Yow-ow-ow-ow-ow ... Yipe!' I guessed that the Boss had asked her to be quiet.

'Got shot – I knew he would,' says Floosie. 'Bark got into bad company like meself. Ah well, he hadn't much sense.' She gave Gwilym a lick. 'You'd better go home and comfort the mother of your puppies,' says she.

THIRTY-FIVE

BARK was killed in a shooting accident. He happened to be crossing a field where some stray dogs were worrying sheep. He was in the calf house when I got home, lying in state.

Mr O'Brien was in the yard with the Boss and Yank. Mr O'Brien had put Bark in a timber kennel with a ten foot high wire paling and he didn't tie him up. Too much of the chain is bad, and besides, his neck was sore. Bark ate his way out in minutes. He met up with other dogs and I've told the rest. Mr O'Brien said he should have minded him better. He made a mistake, he said, and only for him, Bark would be living yet. He wanted to pay Yank back.

'Forget about the bet,' says the Boss. 'You hadn't Bark long enough to train him.' Yank sat on a bale of hay and said his back was paining him.

'I don't know what you gave for Bark,' says Mr O'Brien, 'not very much, I imagine.' (Yank shivered.) 'I hope you won't be at any loss if I give you this puppy.' The puppy was a daughter of his Mist, nine months old. 'She's working nicely,' says he. 'Her name is Meg. If there's anything else I can do, you've only to ask.'

Yank was delighted. He was near forgetting poor

Bark, lying cold and stiff in the calf house. 'If that be the case,' says he, 'would you be so kind as to bury Bark?' Yank's back won't let him dig graves, and neither will the Boss's hernia, but I got the impression that Mr O'Brien wasn't expecting that job. The grave is beside Dolly's at the end of the potato rows.

Mr O'Brien took Meg back with him. Yank asked him to give her a bit of training. He must be wishing he never made the offer of help. The Boss was raging with Yank and offered Mr O'Brien one of Floosie's pups. 'Thank you, Jack,' says he, 'I think I have dogs enough just now.' He drove away in a hurry.

When he was gone, the Boss attacked Yank over taking Meg off him and then asking him to train her. 'Bark wasn't worth fourpence, and you know it,' says he, 'and he wasn't even your dog to my way of thinking. Jim Dolan was his rightful owner.'

'I can go back to New York,' says Yank, 'and take me dog. There's no quarantine, I inquired.' Then he turned as white as Floosie. 'Is there any phone nearer than Coolcoffin?' says he. 'Upon me oath, when I look around me, I'm hardly able to believe I was reared in such a backward place.'

'You were reared here all right,' says the Boss, 'and our Mammy, God be good to her, was only wasting her time with you. What do you want with a phone all in a rush?'

Yank didn't answer. He jumped in the car, and missed me by an inch as he raced out of the yard.

I found Jess whining in the haybarn. 'The Boss struck me,' says she, 'when I was mourning for our friend, and me in my condition.'

I was surprised. 'Are you?' says I. 'I thought you said you were having a rest.'

'There's no rest for a good bitch like me,' says Jess, and she began, very softly, to sing Bark's favourite song: 'Take these chains from me neck and set me free . . .'

✤

When the place was robbed, and Yank's clothes and his camera was taken, he was boasting about how clever he was, wearing a belt with all his dollars in it. 'I can easy buy another coat,' says he. It wasn't until he had the row with the Boss and said he'd go back to New York that he remembered that his passport and his return ticket was in his coat pocket. So now we have the guards back here and Yank carrying on a fright.

In the middle of it all, word came that Martin could be brought home from hospital, so Julia and the Boss went to get him. They let me go too, and I was very curious to see him in his collar and maybe a lead. It comes of not being educated; I'm always making mistakes. I was glad I hadn't said anything to Floosie about the collar. It's a big white yoke, made of plastic or something, and it isn't to tie him up by or lead him around, it's to keep his head on. I did notice though, that he had a name tag – I have a name tag as well.

When I got over the shock of seeing Martin with his head fastened on with a plastic collar, I began to wonder what would Julia say after the way she's been giving out about him. Well, I've said it before, people is strange creatures, you couldn't be up to them. Julia took a run at Martin, put the two arms around him and said he was her own darling husband what she was mad about. Martin looked fairly pleased. 'All right, all right. Mind me neck,' says he. I was in mortal dread for the safety of his head.

When we got back to his house, Julia led him inside by his arm, talking all the time about how she missed him every minute and how Peejay missed him too. Yank was there, minding Peejay, who is growing a new lot of teeth. He was whining and dribbling like a bulldog.

When everyone was gone inside, I went to see Floosie. The puppies were running around and she was sitting up in the hayrack where they couldn't reach her. 'I'm weaning them,' says she. 'Did you hear any word of the Boss finding homes for them?'

'I did,' says I. 'Jim Dolan is getting Gwilym and Boosie, on account of losing Bark, Dylan's going to Colonel Crankshaft to keep Tiny company, the Missis wants to keep little Lark herself, and Ceri and Evan are going to be guide dogs for the blind.'

Floosie laughed so much, she fell out of the hayrack, and the puppies all made for her at once. She snarled at them and jumped back out of reach. 'Guide dogs,' says she, still laughing.

'Julia's all about Martin now,' says I. 'She's in the kitchen sitting on his lap, and the two of them is eating bread and butter. What changed her, I wonder?'

'Euphoria Ryan won in Dublin last night, with Dominic Molumphy singing Martin's song,' says Floosie. 'Martin is getting money for the song, and Dominic is getting Euphoria for a prize, I heard. They're going to America with the Sobsisters on a tour.'

'I didn't think you could win a person for a prize,' says I.

'I don't see why not,' says Floosie. 'Me Granny

152

was offered as second prize in a raffle once. A bank manager won her, but there was a choice of her or £20 and he took the cash.'

'Maybe this Dominic will take cash instead of the Euphoria one,' says I.

'Not a chance,' says Floosie.

I thought I'd better be getting home. Jess is inclined to howl when I'm away, and I didn't want the Boss to strike her again. Jess is very sensitive – it's on account of being so well bred, she says. She tells me her skin is so sensitive she'd feel a thistle through half a bale of straw. That's why she doesn't like working unless the ground is clean and dry, and no thistles.

It must be troublesome to be as well bred as that.

THIRTY-SIX

TWO different guards came down to our farm today. They had raincoats on them and plain hats, but they smelled like guards to me. One of them banged on the door and the Missis came out. 'Is Patrick Jeremiah Kelly staying here?' says he.

'He is not,' says the Missis, then she remembered that Patrick Jeremiah Kelly is Yank's name, so she says, 'Oh, Paddy, yes he is – or no, he isn't, he's staying at me son's but he's here.' The guard gave her a funny look and wrote something down in a book. Yank came out from the settee in the best room; he'd been resting after a hard couple of hours at the pub.

'I suppose there isn't any chance that you've found Chris,' says he, in a nasty voice.

The guard looked in his book. 'Are you referring to Christopher Pascal Muldoon?' says he, 'because if you are, no we haven't, but we've found out that Patrick Jeremiah Kelly, staying with his brother John William Kelly at Wisheen, Coolcoffin, Co Galway, returned to New York via Shannon Airport last Friday.'

Yank looked as if he might have a fit or faint. He sat down and put his head in his hands. 'I'm ruined,' says he.

'Ruined how are you?' says the Missis. 'You have money and your health – you should be thankful for what you have.' She sounded a bit like Jess.

They talked it out all ways, but there was nothing to be done. Yank looks like staying for ever, and nobody will miss Chris except Floosie. When the guards was gone, the Boss, the Missis and Yank sat around the table while I lay underneath. The Missis had just said she'd make some tea when we heard another car. 'We have nothing only traffic,' says the Boss, 'we might as well be living in Dublin.'

The Missis looked out. 'Oh Mother of God,' says she. 'What'll we do now? It's Mrs O'More who bought the last litter of pups. She might be bringing them back, and they must be six months old at least.'

'Talk to her you,' says the Boss. 'It was you sold them to her.' He went into the best room and shut the door after him.

Mrs O'More had on a black dress, and nearly as many chains around her neck as Bark. 'My dear Kathleen,' says she, 'how very nice to meet you again.'

'Thanks,' says the Missis, looking nervous. 'Paddy, this is Mrs O'More that got the eight pups. Paddy's Jack's brother from the States.'

'Majella,' says Mrs O'More, 'don't you dare call me Mrs.' She gave Yank a big smile and shook him by the hand. 'Delighted to meet you, Paddy.'

Yank half got up and muttered something, then he sat down again.

The Missis was getting over the shock by degrees. 'Sit down,' says she, 'I'll wet the tea.' I edged further under the table. Majella smelled like flowers – strong ones – and I never did care for gardening. She didn't see me. Soon they were all talking away, Paddy this,

155

Majella that, Kathleen the other. I wondered at them. Then they went out to see Jess.

I went too, and Majella was talking to Yank and didn't look where she was going. She nearly fell, because she was wearing those high shoes they put on women to keep them from running away. Then she noticed me, and gave me a big hug. 'This must be Daddy,' says she, 'he's just like his family. Come along Shep, we'll go and see Mummy, shall we?'

I went under the henhouse, the smell of flowers was terrible and I couldn't get rid of it. I didn't come out until I heard Majella driving away.

Majella

'That lady knows a top class brood bitch when she sees one,' says Jess, 'she has the whole of me next litter booked.'

'What did she do with the last ones?' says I.

'They went to a famous trials man,' says Jess. 'What with me being so well bred, nothing would do him but to buy them all.'

'I'm well bred too,' says I.

'I know, Shep,' says Jess. 'It's a shame you only have a blue certificate instead of a pink one like mine.'

I was vexed. 'Your pink certificate isn't much addition when an old ewe stamps her foot at you,' says I. 'You run away so fast you have no time to remember what colours your papers are.'

Jess pretended not to hear. 'Stop bothering me,' says she, 'I need me rest at a time like this.'

THIRTY-SEVEN

MAJELLA didn't go back to Dublin; she stayed at the Hurlers' Rest in Coolcoffin. It isn't a great place to stay. We all thought she had an old husband somewhere, but Jess says she buried him two years back. She has no dogs now, and every time she sees one, she carries on like Julia's friends do over Peejay. Most of all, she loves Jess. Jess is crazy about Majella, because she loves being petted and stroked. She sits beside Majella when she comes here, which is often, and lays her chin on her knee. Majella sits by the hour, scratching her head (Jess's head, I mean of course) while she talks to the Missis and Yank. Me and the Boss keep out of the way; Jess tells me about it.

All Floosie's puppies have gone except Jenkyn. Floosie is growing her coat and the scabs on her face have healed. She told me that Martin lost his voice when he broke his neck. Julia was pretending she minded. He still has his collar. Last week, he went on a guided tour of a new abattoir, which Jess tells me is some kind of a supermarket. He'd won £500 for his song and he said he'd bring Julia and Peejay a present they wouldn't forget.

That day, Majella called at our house as she usually does, and found Yank sitting outside, staring at the

Gombeen Hills and doing nothing. 'Would you like a drive to Salthill, Paddy?' says she. 'The sea air is gorgeous.'

'I will flying,' says Yank, jumping up. Then, if you'll believe me, Majella decided that Jess would like to go for the ride. Jess hasn't been in a car since she came here, but Majella called her and she came wagging up to her. She put her arms around Jess and lifted her into the car.

'Upsy pupsy!' says she. 'My word, there are lots of little puppy-wuppies there, aren't there, my Jessie?' They drove away. I went around to the back of the haybarn and was sick.

Martin got home first. He had a big case with him, and Julia made sure it was her present, but it was bagpipes. Martin thought if he couldn't sing, he'd make some other noise. He had a fiddle, but Julia stepped on it by accident.

Much later, Yank and Majella came home. Jess went into the stable in a hurry and dug herself into the straw. 'I don't think much of this old driving,' says she. 'I might have had a miscarriage; I was sick.'

'So was I,' says I.

❁

'Yank and Majella is getting married,' says Jess to me next day.

'You're dreaming,' says I. 'Yank's near as old as the Boss.'

'It was a whirlwind romance,' says Jess. 'Majella suddenly knew Yank was the Only One – it was him or nobody. You wouldn't understand, Shep.'

I didn't. Majella is twice Yank's size and weight, but she's a puppy beside him when it comes to age.

159

Yank had to get a licence (I have a licence too) and they got married in Dublin. 'You can have Floosie's last pup for a wedding present,' says the Missis. 'He's a dote.'

Yank looked at Jenkyn, and Jenkyn stared hard back at Yank. Yank looked away. 'Thank you Kathleen,' says he, 'but no. He reminds me of poor Bark – I'd feel sad every time I looked at him.'

'What will we give you so?' says the Missis. I don't know Majella that well, but I know she's cracked about dogs.'

'I know what she'd like,' says Yank. 'Would you think of parting with Jess? When she has her litter reared, of course.'

The Missis wasn't sure, but the Boss thought it was a great idea. 'We have Floosie now,' says he, 'she can't follow Chris to America and she's twice the dog Jess ever was.' He's getting sense at last.

'What about breeding?' says the Missis. 'Her papers is lost.'

'We'll get copies or get her registered on merit. The trial men would be queuing up for pups off Shep and Floosie.'

Floosie and Jenkyn are staying here, because Martin is learning the bagpipes and it's too much for them. Julia and Peejay is staying with Julia's Mammy. Jenkyn is the boldest pup I ever saw, but Floosie takes no notice. 'I believe in trying anything once,' says she. 'I've reared one litter and that's it. I'll have no more. As for Jenkyn, the sooner they get rid of him the better.'

Jess is disgusted with Floosie. 'Jenkyn's a grand little fellow,' says she. 'Maybe a little high-spirited. He needs love and understanding.'

160

'I understand him,' says Floosie, 'that's why I don't love him – and don't get excited, Jess. Remember the seven or eight tiny lives you are carrying.'

'That's the first decent thing you ever said to me,' says Jess.

Jim Dolan came to mind us dogs while the family was at the wedding. He has his two pups sold, and he took a fancy to Jenkyn, so the Boss said he could keep him for his trouble. 'Serve him right,' says Floosie. 'It was him brought Bark out of Wales.'

Yank and Majella are going to live in a new house near Dublin. They are going to breed Border Collies and Yorkshire terriers. Jess is thrilled to be going to live near the city; she is to go when her pups are reared in about eight weeks. They are due tomorrow. 'I'm to be the cornerstone of Yank's enterprise,' says she. 'At last I've found me vocation. Me and my puppies will found a new dynasty.'

'What's that?' says I.

'It's a lot of good dogs. I'll be remembered along with Johnny Wilson's Peg, Thomas Longton's Bess, and a host of immortal bitches.'

I was glad she was so pleased. I'll miss her meself. She could always explain hard words to me, and you'd know what she'd be thinking. I never know what Floosie's thinking. 'Won't you be sorry to leave us, Jess?' says I.

'In a way I will,' says Jess, 'but I owe it to meself to move on to higher things. Majella lets me sit on her lap.'

Then the Missis came and took Jess away to the calf house where Bark lay in state and where all our puppies have been born.

❀   ❀   ❀   ❀

161

I think I have enough written about me and the Boss and the Missis.

I think I'll write no more. It isn't natural for a dog.

I think from now on, I'll stick to working the cattle and sheep, with maybe an odd run at the trials.

Last night, Jess had six pups. They are as black as ink.

Shep. Coolcoffin 1993.

OTHER FARMING PRESS PUBLICATIONS

A Way of Life: H GLYN JONES & BARBARA COLLINS
Sheepdog Training, Handling and Trialling

A complete guide to sheepdog work and trialling, in which Glyn Jones' life is presented as an integral part of his tested and proven methods.

Come Bye! and Away!   H GLYN JONES
VHS colour video

Glyn Jones demonstrates the basic sheepdog training techniques focusing on the moment when a young dog is first let off the leash in a field of sheep and learns to obey the four commands.

That'll Do!   H GLYN JONES
VHS colour video

Sequel to the above video, in which Glyn Jones teaches more specific commands and then reduces command contact.

Country Dance   HENRY BREWIS

A contemporary fable of a family farm and the changes it has witnessed over the past 60 years.

Don't Laugh Till He's Out of Sight   HENRY BREWIS

Henry Brewis's early stories (with some cartoons and verses).

The Spacious Days   MICHAEL TWIST

An account of growing up on an estate at Burnham in Buckinghamshire in the 1920s and '30s—humorous, informative and imbued with a love of the countryside.

For more information or for a free illustrated list giving full details of our wide range of agricultural and veterinary books, please contact:

Farming Press Books & Videos, Wharfedale Road, Ipswich IP1 4LG, United Kingdom
Telephone (0473) 241122   Fax (0473) 240501

Farming Press Books is part of the Morgan-Grampian Farming Press Group which publishes a range of farming magazines: *Arable Farming, Dairy Farmer, Farming News, Pig Farming, What's New in Farming.* For a specimen copy of any of these please contact the address above.